THE CUSTOM

1911

BILL LOËB

Published by

Gun Digest® Books, an imprint of F+W, A Content + eCommerce Company
Krause Publications • 700 East State Street • Iola, WI 54990-0001
715-445-2214 • 888-457-2873
www.krausebooks.com

To order books or other products call toll-free 1-800-258-0929
or visit us online at www.gundigeststore.com

Cover photography by Yamil Sued

ISBN-13: 978-1-4402-4055-3
ISBN-10: 1-4402-4055-8

Design by Dane Royer
Edited by Jennifer L.S. Pearsall

Printed in China

ACKNOWLEDGEMENTS

Putting a book together takes a lot of effort and help from a lot of people. There were dozens of shooters, inventors, businessmen, and manufacturers, as well as, office personnel and historians who helped. Many did so because they believed in the project, others because it was their job. The majority helped just because they are nice people, the kind of folks the gun culture is filled with.

It is fair to say that there is no way I can name them all, and I shan't try, save two. Those two people are Jennifer L.S. Pearsall and Carol Finnigan.

Jennifer is a dear friend. She envisioned this project and, more importantly, believed in me. If it were not for her, I would not have had the opportunity. The words, "Thank you" do not seem adequate.

Carol Finnigan was my assistant through this project. She worked tirelessly, kept crazy hours, and spent a ton of time organizing, transcribing, scheduling, emailing, and otherwise keeping things going. In addition to her workload, she was also inspirational. When I would be discouraged, she would not let me stay down. Were it not for her, there is no way that I could have delivered this to the publisher on time. Perhaps I never could have done it. This book deserves to have her name on the cover as much as mine.

PREFACE

There is a funny thing about writing a book; it goes where it wants to, not necessarily where you expect it to go.

When I was first approached about this project, I must admit, I was dubious. After all, does the world really need another 1911 book? Haven't enough people with far more expertise than I already pontificated about it?

It took more than a couple of weeks of consideration. My editor, Jennifer Pearsall, would find any excuse to call me. She used the fabricated opportunities to cajole me into taking the project. I appreciated her support, but didn't want to be just another writer blowing hot air.

Finally, I agreed to write the book, because I thought I had come up a unique angle. Pat Sweeney had just recently released his outstanding book, *The 1911—The First 100 Years*. I thought that writing a follow up would be a good idea, one explaining where the gun presently exists in its development and to lay out where it would be going over the next 100 years. That didn't happen.

My research began with me approaching many prominent people in the 1911 world, be they small craftsmen, competitive shooters, hunters, manufacturers, or inventors. As a group, they welcomed me with open arms, giving me unprecedented access. I was humbled by their kindness and made more than one friend along the way. I can tell you that there are some wonderful things going on behind the scenes, and I truly wish I could share all of them with you. Sadly, due to proprietary concerns, a book about the next 100 years of 1911 development isn't going to happen.

As I continued to investigate, interview, and shoot with these folks, I realized that the 1911 itself isn't really the story. It never has been. We all know the gun and what it is about.

John Moses Browning was a brilliant man and his design was spectacular. That firearm masterpiece has been the catalyst for bringing together some truly brilliant people. They form a confederation of sorts, a subculture among shooters and gun collectors in general. They are a group of people brought together by their common love for the 1911. They are not unlike that of the fans of Harley Davidson. The bikes are what they are, largely unchanged for decades. Their fans, however, come from every walk of life, every socioeconomic stratum, brought together by their focus on those bikes and those bikes only. Their mutual interest and love for the brand are what bring them together.

Of course, the 1911 isn't a brand. It is a design now manufactured by an amazingly large number of companies. From the one-man shop to one of the most high-tech manufacturing companies in the world, they share admiration for John Moses Browning's masterpiece. In these pages, you will meet a man who needed to boost the morale of his company, so he began producing his workers' favorite gun. Now this company makes the world's most precise 1911. You will learn about one of the world's greatest female shooters who started her amazing shooting career with a 1911 simply because it fit her hand. One fellow was a successful competitive shooter who used his fame shooting the 1911 as a platform to launch the largest custom 1911 shop in the world.

There are many, many more. Of course, there are too many stories for one book and you will surely notice some omissions. Some people were too busy in this prosperous time in the gun business. Others were, well, let me just say that some of them are their own biggest fans and do not feel the need to explain to the world why they are so extremely awesome.

I did my best to let the people in this book tell their stories in their own voice. Some needed no help; others were reluctant to recount their tales. In the end, I hope it is their personalities that shine through.

The 1911 is what brought them together.

And they are your people.

ABOUT THE AUTHOR

Bill Loëb is a lifelong gun enthusiast, having purchased his first gun at age nine; firearms have always been a driving force in his life. His association with the 1911 began when he was 18 and got his first semi-automatic handgun, a Colt Combat Commander. Currently, Bill enjoys all the gun games including IDPA, USPSA, and Falling Steel matches.

An avid reader himself, Bill has previously been published in a variety of newspapers and periodicals, and he also had a popular show on talk radio.

Bill taught his daughter to respect and handle firearms at a young age and took her shooting with him before she was six years old. Understanding the importance of personal safety Bill also teaches women and children self-defense.

INTRODUCTION

It seems like every book about the 1911 starts out the same way. Talking about how it's the most iconic gun in history or how it has stood the test of time like no other. It also seems there's the inevitable discussion about how John Browning was the smartest man who ever lived, a genius for the ages.

Blah, blah, blah.

Yes, we all know John Moses Browning never woke up dumb a day in his life, and, yes, the 1911 is one of the most recognizable handguns ever produced. This book isn't about that. There are plenty of historians who are happy to tell you about every incarnation of the 1911 throughout the last century. I am not they.

This book is about what is happening *now* in the world of 1911s, because there have never been so many choices for the 1911 enthusiast. Why? Because genius loves company. Since its introduction, some great minds have developed that military workhorse into one of the finest pistols one can own, no matter what the purpose or desire.

Let's look at some of those great ideas. The long slide was created by Jim Clark. It seemed he came across a drum of "de-milled" slides that had been cut just so; he used them to produce slides longer than the originals. In addition, Jim saw the benefit of the stabilizing the end of the barrel more than a standard bushing could. His coned insert supported the barrel muzzle with unheard of security and precision. Ed Brown sawed off the back of the grip, creating the "bobtail," which made concealing the gun much easier. Para-Ordnance produced a viable double-stack 1911. Okay, you caught me, John Moses actually might have come up with that one, since he had already used a staggered magazine in the Browning Hi-Power—but you get the point. That simple yet brilliant design has evolved in meaningful ways. John Browning would be amazed.

Development is only a positive thing if it leads to greater performance. Consider that, according to the Army, John Browning's original gun had an "effective range" of 50 yards. That means you had a reasonably good chance of hitting a man at that range. Bring that forward to today, where Hayes Custom Guns builds a 1911 that shoots two-inch groups at 50 yards. Now, I do not know how many square inches a man is, but that is a startling improvement over the original.

No doubt your granddaddy shakes his head when he sees an aluminum-framed 1911, but consider that his gun probably rode on a strong belt under a flap holster. If you carry concealed every day, a 38-ounce gun gets pretty tiresome. On the other hand, an Adventurer variation produced by the craftsmen at Cylinder & Slide is a joy to carry. Weighing in at a mere 25 ounces it is a tidy package.

I could go on and on, but you get the idea. Constant development has led to a 1911 that is still the best choice for countless applications.

The United States Marine Corps Special Operations Command needed to find a sidearm for their quick reaction forces, their Marine Expeditionary Unit, or MEU, and the brass there turned to none other than the 1911. Outward appearances might indicate it is the same pistol carried by their predecessors at Iwo Jima and Tarawa. While most of the parts would interchange, the improvement of those parts makes the modern incarnation a far more accurate and ergonomic sidearm.

Who else considers the modern 1911 their best option? The Los Angeles Police Department S.W.A.T. (Special Weapons and Tactics) team carries Kimber Custom TLEs (Tactical Law Enforcement.) The Federal Bureau of Investigations arms its S.W.A.T. and H.R.T. (Hostage Rescue Team) with 1911s from the Springfield Custom Shop. How about the United States Army's counter-terrorism unit, the 1st Special Forces Operational Detachment-Delta? You guessed it, Delta Force uses a 1911. Of course, "snake eaters" are a secretive lot and do all of their modifications in underground bunkers that have armed guards and razor wire. Still, it doesn't take a Ouija board to figure out that their guns are similar or identical to those of other specialized warriors.

The 1911 has always been known for toughness and reliability and even those attributes have seen improvement. World Champion competitive shooter Todd Jarrett took an unmodified Para-Ordnance and shot 1,000 rounds in 10 minutes and 44 seconds; the barrel reached a temperature in excess of 550 degrees. Todd maintains that, if had he not bobbled a few magazines and had those magazine all been of the same capacity, he could have gotten below the 10-minute mark. That is not the end of the story. He and some other shooters put *5,000* rounds through the gun, just to prove its toughness. It ran like a champ. No failure to feed. No failure to extract. No stovepipes. It just went bang—repeatedly.

The accuracy, reliability, and toughness of today's 1911 is truly a result of constant improvement. Every single part has been upgraded. Just look at the seemingly simple guide rod. It can be standard length or full length. If you select the latter, it can be one-piece or two-piece. Stainless steel or tungsten is your next choice. If you choose tungsten, you usually have three weight options. They all have their advantages, depending upon your need. Is your head spinning yet?

This is all just a hint at what's to come in the following pages. Don't let it intimidate you. The wide variety of options allows the modern 1911 to be perfectly tailored to whatever your mission might be. Well, that is if your mission requires a tough, reliable, accurate pistol that would amaze John Moses Browning himself.

TABLE OF CONTENTS

Acknowledgements..3

Preface 4

About the Author 5

Introduction 6

PART I—IN THE BEGINNING

CHAPTER 1 A Brief History 11

PART II—THE MAKERS

CHAPTER 2 Early Customization 19

CHAPTER 3 Stan Chen: A Passion to Create 23

CHAPTER 4 Cabot: The Story of Unparalleled Precision 32

CHAPTER 5 Republic Forge: The All-American Maker 46

CHAPTER 6 From STI is Born SVI... 50

CHAPTER 7 Luke Volkmann: Delving into the Details 58

CHAPTER 8 Bill Laughridge's Cylinder & Slide
(and all the other important parts, too)............................ 64

CHAPTER 9 Nighthawk: The Rise to the Top 70

CHAPTER 10 Ed Brown: It's Personal 86

CHAPTER 11 Wilson Combat: Once Removed from John Moses 98

CHAPTER 12 Kimber: Saved by the 1911 110

PART III—THE 1911'S SHOOTING STARS

CHAPTER 13 The Games We Play...121

CHAPTER 14 Chip McCormick: Starting at the Top 130

CHAPTER 15 Bruce Piatt: Decades of Winning Ways 139

CHAPTER 16 Scott McGregor: Making 3-Gun History.......................146

CHAPTER 17 Julie Golob: Wonder Woman with a Gun 150

CHAPTER 18 Jesse Tischauer: The New 1911 Kid on the Block.............153

CHAPTER 19 Ted Nugent: Beware the Hunter with a 10mm 1911............157

CHAPTER 20 Razor Dobbs: Handgun Hunting Sensation 162

PART IV—THE MODERN 1911

CHAPTER 21 The Calibers 171

CHAPTER 22 Handloading for the 1911..194

CHAPTER 23 Making the Compact 1911 Right 208

CHAPTER 24 Sights for Your Carry 1911 213

CHAPTER 25 Tactical Lights: Pros and Cons 217

CHAPTER 26 Laser Sights on the Custom 1911.................................... 223

CHAPTER 27 Dry-Firing the Custom 1911: Yes You Can! 226

CHAPTER 28 The 1911 Extractor: It's No Small Thing............................ 229

CHAPTER 29 Common Issues that Sideline Your Custom 1911 231

CHAPTER 30 Required Maintenance.. 234

PART I

IN THE BEGINNING

A BRIEF HISTORY

N THE BEGINNING, JOHN MOSES BROWNING created the 1911… and God saw that it was good.

Before you accuse me of blasphemy, understand that there is no greater deity in the gun world than John Moses Browning. With 128 patents that covered sporting rifles, machine guns, handguns, and shotguns you have to admit, John was every bit the genius they say. Take a look at the following list. There are some pretty amazing guns here, many of which would, all by themselves assure a place in history for their creator.

- 1895 Colt Browning Maching gun
- Model 1899 and 1900 Fabrique Nationale d'Herstal Browing
- Colt Model 1900
- Colt Model 1902
- Colt Model 1903
- Colt Model 1903 hammerless
- Colt Model 1905
- Fabrique Nationale d'Herstal Model 1906 Vest Pocket
- Remington Model 8
- Colt Model 1908 vest pocket
- Colt Model 1908 Hammerless
- Fabrique Nationale d'Herstal 1910
- Colt Woodsman
- Winchester 1885 falling block
- Winchester 1886 lever-action
- Winchester 1897 lever-action
- Winchester 1890 lever-action
- Winchester 1892 lever-action
- Winchester 1894 lever-action
- Winchester 1895 lever-action

The Savage 1907

The Springfield 1911 was designed to be a .22-caliber training gun. This is one of only 25 produced. The project was scrapped by World War I.

1911 manufactured by Union Switch.

- Winchester 1897 lever-action
- Browning Auto 5
- Browning .22 semi-auto
- M1917 water-cooled machine gun
- M1919 air-cooled machine gun
- Browning Automatic
- Rifle (a.k.a. BAR M1918)
- M2 .50-caliber machine gun
- M4 37mm auto cannon
- Fabrique Nationale d'Herstal Trombone pump-action rifle
- Remington Model 8
- Remington Model 24
- Browning Hi-Power
- Browning Superposed over/under shotgun
- Ithaca Model 37 pump-action
- And, of course, the Model 1911 45ACP.

There are many design features that make this pistol unique, not the least of which is the short recoil action. Browning designed the tilting barrel, which allows the barrel and the slide to be locked together for only a short distance during the firing cycle. This is the design principle of virtually all handguns today that are 9mm and larger. (Less powerful handguns are often straight blowback designs.)

That original 1911 was, design wise, virtually identical to the 1911 of today. It seems that Browning had already been working on a short recoil handgun for Colt when Colonel John Thompson (creator of the Thompson Machine Gun, a.k.a. the Tommy Gun), and Colonel Louis LaGarde decided the Army needed a handgun with more stopping power. The .38 Long Colt revolvers had not done the job during battle in the Philippines, and, so, a .45-caliber projectile was mandated. The search for the new military sidearm was on.

The 1911 was not born overnight. It started with the M1900, which was adapted to accept the larger cartridge the Army wanted. That gun became known as the M1905. However, the barrel link wasn't strong enough to handle the more powerful cartridge. Of course, Browning being Browning, he found

a work-around and the gun was soon deemed ready for commercial sale.

The Federal Government wasn't any better at meeting deadlines then than it is now, so the 1906 Trials began in 1907. Seemingly everyone wanted a shot at the prize, but only a handful showed up. Of the seven that threw their hat in the ring, it ended up being a race between three. They were Colt's and Savage, along with Deutsche Waffen- und Munitionsfabriken Aktien-Gesellschaft, known as DWM, maker of the Luger.

It is important to understand that the Army would look at a gun and think, "Wouldn't this be better with a safety?" and then the manufacturers would run off and adapt their design. It was not a case of "run what ya brung," but, rather, adapt to an ever-changing criteria.

Early on, the race for the Army contract was an interesting one. The Savage entrant, the M-1907, was a well-made gun, but it had some issues. One was that the recoil was very stiff. Another was that the controls aren't located in the most ergonomic of places.

Take, for instance, the magazine release. It is small and located in a concavity on the middle of the front of the grip, all the way at the bottom. The end of the pinkie finger is required to release the magazine.

The lanyard loop is perhaps the silliest design element of the Savage pistol, yet there is also a certain elegance to it. It folds down into the magazine well. That's right, the lanyard loop is folded into a recess on the inside rear of the magazine well. It appears like it would work okay. Still, looking at it with modern eyes, where magazine changes are considered among the most important elements of handgunning, anything that could potentially get in the way is frowned upon.

There are other issues with the Savage design. The slide release is engaged by pushing directly up towards the slide with your trigger finger. The safety is hinged at the front, which makes for an activation that disturbs the shooter's grip on the gun. Then there's the rear sight that serves double duty as the extractor, a unique element to say the least. Add to all this the fact that the grip angle is more similar to that of a cordless drill than that of a gun and you have an ergonomic nightmare.

Now before we insult the Savage too much, let us remember that the folks back then were on the frontier, exploring and inventing what would and would not become the next modern pistol. It does not take a great imagination to envision an engineer thinking of the small, difficult to use magazine release as being a benefit. After all, if the magazine release were too accessible, it could lead to ejecting the magazine in the heat of battle.

It wasn't all bad, the Savage had some more sensible design elements. One was a rotating barrel, an inventive system still used today by Beretta, specifically in that company's 8000 series. Yes, most pistols today are patterned after the Browning short action. Still, that the rotating barrel design is in use a century later proves its worth.

The other major player in the game for the Army contract way back when was the Luger. That's right, if things had turned out differently, the Luger might not just have been the gun of the Nazi's but also that of the American G.I. Of course, I'm not giving away the story by telling you that it was not to be.

At the time of the trials, DWM was successfully producing the gun we commonly refer to simply as a Luger, more properly known as the Pistole Parabellum 1908. Designed by an impressive young Austrian named Georg Luger, the gun was chambered in what has become the ubiquitous 9mmx19, a cartridge developed specifically for his gun. DWM already had contracts with the German Navy and the Swiss Army and were on the cusp of having the German Army adopt its handgun, as well, so with good reason they were confident and riding tall in the saddle. Now, remember, the U.S. Army contract had mandated that the new sidearm be cambered in a cartridge of at least .45-caliber. Georg Luger adapted the handgun, although not enthusiastically, for the larger cartridge.

DWM only built two guns to send to the Army for testing. My guess was that it was a half-hearted attempt and the test guns had not been shaken down well, but who knows? The bottom line is that two .45-caliber pistols based on the Luger design were sent with what appeared to be a certain amount of disinterest.

When tested, none of the three entrants did well. The Savage was clearly the leader, but problematic. The Colt and the Luger were tied for a distant second

YAMIL SUED PHOTO

place. The Luger would lock up, something Luger blamed on the ammunition. We may never know if it was truly the ammo or if the trademark Luger "toggle" mechanism, just has too many moving parts for the more powerful cartridge. The Colt would occasionally send a slide downrange along with the bullet. Surely, this was a source of embarrassment.

The leaderboard notwithstanding, the test results made it clear that the Army did not yet have the gun it wanted. More testing was needed, so it offered all three companies a contract to build 200 guns. After some discussion, DWM, who had not been enthusiastic from the beginning, declined. It was already flush with orders in Europe, and, since it had never been fully invested into the

project, bowing out seemed a practical choice. There are other theories. Some felt DWM would never get a fair shake against American manufacturers. Others believe that the company was already overwhelmed with the success of its 9mm pistols in Europe, and simply didn't have the time and resources. No matter what the reason, they ducked the challenge.

Savage and Colt accepted the contract, but their attitudes were quite different. Savage was already producing its 1905 and 1907 pistols, and they were selling well. The disruption in production for only 200 guns seemed an intolerable proposition, so it produced the same gun it had brought to the earlier tests with little or no improvements.

We've come a long way from the 1906 trials.

Colt's approach was a contrast. Mainly a revolver company at the time, it felt the Army contract was a huge opportunity. Not only was Colt's concerned that the wheel-gun had a limited lifespan, it sensed it was falling behind in the country's new pistol market. With these things in mind, John Browning took what he learned from the failures of the early trials and totally redesigned the pistol.

Early on, in order to satisfy the Army's insistence that the gun have a safety of some sort, Browning's solution was the hastily added grip safety. He was not fond of the feature. But the Army wants what it wants, so as he was reworking the gun Browning added a thumb safety. He did this for two reasons. Not only did he opine that it would be looked upon favorably by safety minded Army evaluators, it allowed the gun to be carried safely with a round in the chamber and the hammer back. "Cocked and locked" was born.

It is unknown how much "condition one" or "cocked and locked" helped the 1911 earn adoption as the Army's sidearm, but there is no doubt as to the efficacy and efficiency. One simple move of the thumb, and a clean, crisp, consistent trigger pull awaits the shooter. Of course, the visual of a gun with the hammer back is disturbing to the uninitiated, but the advantages are huge. The quickness and nice trigger pull on the most popular shotguns and rifles are surely due to the rear position of their hammers. (That some hammers can't be seen in their rearward position is a comfort to many.)

The changes to the Colt were numerous, not the least of which was the switch to a single-link locking system. Brown-

ing also became a huge proponent of the coil spring, for its reliability. The bottom line is that the gun that Colt's showed up with, in 1910, was a much improved gun. It was, for all intents and purposes, the 1911 we know today.

Savage, on the other hand, showed up with pretty much the same gun it had brought to the 1907 tests. It was no more reliable or accurate than before. That said, it actually hadn't been all that bad, but with Colt's debut of a much improved gun, the race was about to change.

In the testing, the Savage had done no better than it had before. Broken parts and reliability issues plagued it. The Colt also had issues, not the least of which were cracking frames. The Army gave both another chance and ordered yet another test. Savage finally took the process seriously and worked on its gun, improving it. Colt, meanwhile, beefed up the parts that had broken and fixed the frame problems.

At the end of 1910, Savage and Colt's came back for what would be the final trial, both with guns that ran and ran well. John Browning personally attended the historic torture test. Each gun was fired 100 times and then allowed to cool. It is said that the Colt was dumped in a bucket of water to cool it, which seems like a flamboyant move that John Browning would do. Every thousand rounds, the guns were cleaned and lubed. After what was, at the time, an unheard of 6,000 rounds, the much improved Savage had only 37 malfunctions—but the 1911 had not failed at all. A winner in the race for the Army contract was declared.

We tend to think of WWI as the first place the 1911 saw action, but such was not the case. There was still action in the Philippines, the place that had exposed the weakness of the .38 Long Colt cartridge in the first place. It is said that the 1911 performed well in those continued hostilities. Eventually WWI rolled around, and, yes, the 1911 was there, but here were a lot of young men skeptical of the new-fangled pistol. After all, the boxy gun was unlike anything any Iowa farm boy had ever seen. It didn't take all that long to win them over; despite the abysmal conditions in the trenches, "old slabsides" performed admirably.

Still, there were complaints. The flat mainspring housing was not universally loved and the back edge of the trigger housing was too square for many. The length of the trigger was another point of contention. By 1924, the front sight was wider, the hammer spur longer and reshaped. The grip safety spur was lengthened, grips changed to units with full checkering. The flat mainspring housing was swapped for an arched unit. Other improvements included a shorter trigger and scalloped frame cut outs behind it. Mechanically, the 1911 and the 1911A1 were identical and the parts would interchange, an important benefit that would come into play in the next World War.

Before the fires were put out at Pearl Harbor, the need for a lot of 1911s was clear. The Army was already ramping up, but the "date that will live in infamy" pushed it into top gear. It wasn't long before seemingly everyone was building 1911s: Colt, Remington Rand, Ithaca, H&R, Remington Arms, Union Switch and Signal, Rock Island Arsenal and others. Even Singer, the sewing machine company, made a few hundred.

By the end of the second war to end all wars, nearly two million 1911s had been produced. That was enough that, when the Korean War began, the military had more than enough to go around. It still had plenty on hand to tackle Vietnam.

The military service of the 1911 solidified its popularity, and with good reason. Being hard hitting and dependable is the perfect way for a gun to gain a loyal following. Thousands upon thousands were smuggled home, many simply as souvenirs, but some soldiers simply could not bear to part with the gun that has saved their life. It was those soldiers returning from World War II that created what we think of as the custom 1911. You see, those guys were looking for fun. They souped-up their cars making hot rods out of them. They stripped down motorcycles to make race bikes. As for their guns, those soldiers started modifying them, too—and the transformation of that military workhorse would soon begin in earnest.

PART II

THE MAKERS

EARLY CUSTOMIZATION

THESE DAYS WE HAVE I.D.P.A., U.S.P.S.A, and a plethora of other acronyms, but in the beginning the game was bullseye.

To my knowledge, bullseye is the only shooting sport mandated by law. That's right—law! Title 10 of the United States Code, Section 4312 states:

(a) An annual competition called the "National Matches" and consisting of rifle and pistol matches for a National Trophy, medals and other prizes shall be held as prescribed by the Secretary of the Army.

(b) The National Matches are open to members of the Armed Forces, National Guard, Reserve Officers Training Corps, Air Force Reserve Officers Training Corps, Citizens' Military Training Camps, Citizen's Air Training Camps, and rifle clubs and to civilians.

(c) A Small Arms Firing School shall be held in connection with the National Matches.

(d) Competition for which trophies and medals are provided by the National Rifle Association of America shall be held in connection with the National Matches.

The NRA National Championships have a rich history, and the 1911 really made its presence felt in the grand competition's post-WWII era. With a ton of surplus guns on hand and the many having been smuggled home by G.I.s, it was a natural to modify the 1911 for bullseye.

An elegant version of a Fitz-style open trigger guard

A .38 Special MK III Government Model

The way bullseye works is simple. You have three guns, pistol or revolver, chambered in .22 rimfire, .32-caliber or larger, and a .45-caliber. The course of fire is pretty simple. First there is the "slow-fire" match, in which the competitor has 10 minutes to shoot 10 shots at a range of 50 yards. Next up is the "timed-fire" stage. At a range of 25 yards, strings of five shots must be completed in 20 seconds. The "rapid-fire" stage is exactly the same as the timed-fire, but the time is cut in half for each string, thus allowing 10 seconds for each. This is course of fire is shot three times, once with the .22 rimfire, once with the .32 or larger centerfire and once with the .45 centerfire.

Most competitors just use a .22 pistol and a 1911 in .45ACP, the latter ful-filling the requirements for both the .32-caliber and .45-caliber divisions. This saves money on equipment. This is not to say that some do not use .32s created specifically for the purpose of bullseye; Walther, Benelli and Pardini, as well as others, produce .32s just for the sport. These fine .32s notwithstanding, the 1911 chambered in .45 ACP rules the roost. As I said, in the post-World War II era, there was an abundance of surplus 1911s, as well as tens of thousands smuggled home by G.I.s. It wasn't long before gunsmiths were customizing them.

One of them was a fellow named Jim Clark. He had been a Marine in the Pacific, a tough duty tour on its own, but Clark was also a scout/sniper. He had been assigned to the newly formed 4th Division, which had the distinction of being the first to go directly into battle from the United States. Jim saw action at

A.E. Berdon. Left: Detail of an old added muzzle weight.

a tiny pair of islands named Roi-Namur. When I say tiny, I mean Roi was 1,250 yards at its widest part and Namur was 900 yards—yet they had more than 3,000 Japanese soldiers defending them.

The U.S. Navy pounded the islands, before the Marines landed; there was a shocking number still alive to resist. After securing those islands, Clark was among those sent to Saipan. His Springfield 1903 was damaged along the way, so he scrounged an M1 and some optics. He spotted some Japanese troops trying to escape the invading Marines over a thousand yards away. Once he found his groove, he had over 300 hits.

Surviving a gunshot wound while sav-

ing a buddy, Clark spent months rehabilitating a paralyzed arm before he was discharged. A couple years later, back in Shreveport and going to school, a friend invited him to go to a bullseye match. He promptly borrowed the required guns and learned the rules. In his very first match, he scored a 78 percent. He'd enjoyed it much and decided to pursue the sport. When he went to his first match sponsored by the National Rifle Association, he qualified as a Sharpshooter. His next match he qualified as an Expert. His next match a Master. Unworldly ability.

If bullseye had a rock star, it was Jim Clark. Everything about him seemed bigger than life. (Indeed, he and Bill Blankenship were arguably the greatest civilian bullseye shooters in history.) As Clark's reputation grew and his name continued to appear in the record books, more and more people approached him to buy his guns. If such requests happened after a match, he would gladly sell his pistols for a nice profit, then return home and use his gunsmithing prowess to build more for the next match. When a friend loaned him the money to set up shop, Jim's reputation as a shooter made him an instant success. As the only civilian-trained shooter to win the National Bullseye Championship, his guns were in high demand.

Now, many men would set about to making guns and be content to ride their own reputations into the sunset. Not Jim. His innovations and inventions were numerous. One of Clark's innovations was the long slide. He had been thinking about how to add more weight to the muzzle and elongate the sight ra-

Obregon manufactured an innovative version of the 1911.

dius. Most people were hanging weights off the sides of their guns and adding front sight extensions that pushed the front sights forward of the muzzle. Jim didn't like those ideas, so, when he came across a barrel of slides at an Army surplus store, he bought them all for a dime a piece. With these, he would cut the slide of another gun and extend it. This accomplished everything he wanted, both a longer sight radius and a more muzzle-heavy gun. To Jim, he was just finding a way to get the job done, but, thanks to his creativity, we now call him a visionary.

Of course, while an innovator and a genius in his own right, Jim Clark is also a man who helped other gunsmiths. It is safe to say that his reach went far beyond the guns that came through his shop, Clark Customs, and, today, it is difficult to find a gunsmith who doesn't have appreciation for the man. Truly, here is where one can consider the custom 1911 to have been born.

© NATIONAL FIREARMS MUSEUM

STAN CHEN: A PASSION TO CREATE

FOR STAN CHEN, THERE IS NO OTHER gun except the 1911. Never has been, never will be. Building custom 1911s is all he wants to do.

His passion for the gun started early. As a young lad, about 12 years old, he was always outdoors, hunting, fishing, and often working at his family's ranch in Northern California. He wasn't a big kid, but he carried a big gun, an L-frame S&W .357 with a six-inch barrel. He thought it looked ridiculous, because the barrel hung down to his knee, but he liked carrying the gun and driving the tractor. However, even though it was fun, it wasn't the gun he wanted. He wanted a 1911.

"I would spend all weekend pulling barbed wire, checking on fences, and digging trenches in 104 degree heat, just so I could shoot two mags through my step-dad's Colt Government Model 1911," he told me.

Pretty cheap labor, but Stan was okay with the pay.

"The whole weekend, just searing in the hot sun I was thinking, *Okay, I have 14, 15 rounds here, what am I going to do with 'em? Maybe today I'm gonna see what it does to a 4x4 block.*"

The allure of the 1911 had permeated his consciousness.

"There is just something about that gun. I love the way it looks, balances, handles, and shoots. It just always looked and felt correct to me. The length of the barrel relative to the frame, the clean lines, and perfect location of every control on the pistol. There's something about the 1911 that just always fascinated me.

Beauty and function.

No detail is too small for Stan Chen.

It didn't help that he was a voracious reader, especially of his favorite author, 1911 disciple Col. Jeff Cooper. It was the 1980s, then, and Stan was also reading about current-day shooting heroes who were, of course, 1911 shooters.

"It seemed Brian Enos, Jerry Barnhart, Rob Leatham were in every gun magazines of the day."

The heft, the feel of the safety under his thumb, and more, the gun appealed to him on every level.

"What John Browning created more than 100 years ago still endures as the most ergonomic way to design a pistol for efficient shooting and carry. The consistent single-action trigger is still the best for making accurate, fast hits under stress. It is amazing that it has remained the best for all these years. It is simply what I want to put into my holster."

Young Stan graduated from high school and did what he was supposed to do. He went to the University of California, Los Angeles, and earned a degree. His 1911 dreams got put on hold then, but it didn't stop him from shooting. He shot international pistol for the U.C.L.A pistol team. He also discovered that he loved metallurgy and machining. Because of this, he was always trying to sneak into the machine shop on campus. During this time, Stan met Don Nygord, Olympian shooter in men's free pistol and air pistol events.

"Don would create things, right in his garage, that worked on the big stage. It was inspirational."

After graduation, Stan went to work in corporate life and worked long and

hard. It was what was expected of him as the U.S.-born son of immigrant parents. He did it and he did it well. But it didn't fulfill him.

He met a beautiful blonde with blue eyes and convinced her to marry him. It wasn't long before they had a child on the way. As he approached his thirtieth birthday he recognized that instead of being the happiest time of his life, he was simply miserable.

"I remember the moment when it all came to a head. It was a December night, when I told Kristen, 'I just can't do this anymore.'"

She listened to him as he revealed to her his need for a change, how he had long dreamed of building custom 1911s.

Stan's hand polishing is everywhere.

"She looked at me and said, "Every man needs a life's work. If this is yours, you must do it. I am behind you 100 percent."

Even though his dream had been locked away, indeed, so tightly he had not even read an *American Handgunner* in years, he found himself selling his house and buying equipment for a shop. As luck would have it, a machinist was retiring and needed to dump his tools.

"He had his RV packed and he told me that he had to have the place cleaned out by Sunday. I didn't even know what some of the things were I was buying."

To this day, he finds tools he didn't know that he'd bought in that transaction.

For all of his interest, he didn't have a lot of knowledge at first.

"I didn't know a spindle from a collet, so, for the next few weeks, I was asking advice and making mistakes!"

He also made the mistake of taking a gunsmithing class.

"As I have honed my skills and developed my own specialized methods, tools, and processes, I can honestly tell you that I do not do anything the way I was taught in that class. Trust me, there is not a ballpeen hammer on my bench."

Stan's level of perfectionism is impressive, although he calls it a disease.

"I just don't know when to stop. I can spend the better part of a day fitting a thumb safety, just tuning its feel. How does it feel when it goes up, how does it feels when it goes down. How does it feel at the end of the stroke? Is it completely without over-travel? Does it crisply yet smoothly snap out of the detent?"

Stan spends more time on just the safety than most gunsmiths spend on an entire action job.

The result is a gun that just feels different than any other 1911 you will ever pick up. One particular collector called

Stan and said that he had taken apart a lot of his guns and lain the parts on the bench, all custom guns from famous companies. He wanted to know why Stan's gun had a barrel throat that was different from the others. Then he started asking about the frame cuts. The he asked about the sear. He said to Stan, "All of their gun parts look the same, but every part of your gun is different, sometimes in obvious ways, sometimes subtle."

Stan is a passionate perfectionist. He told me, "It's really difficult for me to know when to stop. I am always pushing myself to do it a little bit better than the last one."

One of Stan's customers has a ritual. When it has been a bad day, he goes into his office, closes the door, and dry-fires a gun that he bought from Chen. He says that the silky smoothness of how the gun feels is a stress reliever.

Because of his attention to detail, Stan rarely completes more than a gun per month. I can say that I have never heard of a gunmaker who spends more time on each gun. What is really telling, though, is that, if he could, he would spend even more time.

"I have to tell you, it is hard to ship a gun to a customer. I have put so much of my heart and soul into them, they are like my children, and I want to keep them for myself."

Stan's wife Kristen said that every man needs a life's work. Stan found his. And he is loving it.

Unique checkering is a
Chen Custom specialty.

A Cabot National Standard

CHAPTER 4

CABOT: THE STORY OF UNPARALLELED PRECISION

WHAT DO YOU GET FROM a group of gun people producing some of the most precision parts ever made? You get the 1911 of Cabot guns.

Cabot Is a division of Penn United Technologies, a manufacturing company that supports many industries. Nuclear power companies, for instance, depend on them, as do defense contractors, the medical industry, and various electronics and telecommunications firms. Yep, if you need precision manufacturing done, you know of Penn United.

Let's just say you have a part you need to manufacture for a medical device and it has to be precise—*really* precise. Cabot can build it for you. The folks there work in tolerances of fifty millionths of an inch. Stop and read that again. *Fifty millionths of an inch.* That is the ability to manufacture dust, if you needed some perfectly consistent, identical dust particles for some reason.

So just why does a company that makes such ultra precise parts decide to get into the gun business? In 2008, when the economy really took a hit, things were pretty tough at Penn United. Orders were cancelled, volume slowed. It was a difficult time. While its actual financial future was not in question, the staff was depressed. Very highly skilled people who take precision and science to the level of art get bored easily. What's the best way to raise moral? At least for gun lovers, it's to build out a favorite pistol, the 1911.

The master polisher's hand work is what make the Black Diamond's finish look wet.

The 1911 project was just the shot in the arm Cabot needed. Eyes brightened and steps quickened. Workers were pumped about creating a new 1911, with methods that have never been used.

The first thing its engineers realized is that the 1911 has been assembled, essentially, the same way for a hundred years. Sure, the metallurgy has changed and the methods of parts production have advanced, but the concept that many of the 52 parts are manufactured oversized and have to be fit to one another is ingrained in the firearms industry. The craftsmen at Penn United just don't get that. In addition to the fact that they believe that every part should fit precisely, they know that whenever you fit something by hand there is variation—and variation is something offensive to them. They believe that if John Moses Browning were alive today, he would produce a gun from parts that fit together, not a gun with part that have to be forced together by a gunsmith. Not only does that forcing method produce parts that

are inconsistent, the final product is, too.

The first order of business at Cabot was to take the drawings of the parts and start creating precise specifications so that they fit together, well, without fitting. This was a more difficult than one might think. A huge amount of resources went into this phase. Engineers had to understand why each part is the size and shape that it is and how and where to reconfigure it for the optimum interaction with the other parts. This was complicated by the fact that, when you ask 10 gunsmiths the same question, you might receive up to 14 answers. Each might work, but which one's best?

After many hours and dollars, the artisans were ready to start. The results are amazing. Just look at the slide-to-frame fit. If you look at any slide under a microscope, you will see peaks and valleys. This is a byproduct of hand lapping. Obviously, the slide rides on the peaks. As the gun wears, those peaks wear down. The smaller the surface area of the peak, the quicker it will wear, simply because there is less material. The rails, on the other hand, due to their advanced grinding techniques, are flat. Truly flat.

This true flatness of the rails does several things. First, it vastly increases the surface area the slide moves on, which means wear is spread out and prolonged. While one cannot say that it does not wear at all (obviously, material is removed by friction), practically speaking, it does not seem to. Brian Zins, former Marine, great shooter, and Cabot Guns evangelist, talks about it all the time. The Cabot slide simply has a smoother, almost ball bearing-like action.

It took a ton of work and the most advanced machining and grinding methods to create what Cabot calls "clone technology," but it has led to a truly interchangeable 1911. If you order any part from slide to sear, it will drop into your Cabot without gunsmithing and do so to factory tolerances.

I mentioned this to a very prominent gunmaker. When I say prominent, I mean, arguably the finest producer in the specific specialty of 1911s. When I told him that the parts on Cabot 1911s were interchangeable, he cried, "Bull squeeze!" In his mind, *that* gentleman is producing the finest, most precise guns on the market. And he is, without question, making guns and parts that are as good and exact as can be made using the equipment, manufacturing methods, and techniques that are available to him. The difference between that creator's very excellent guns and the more excellent guns from Cabot lies in the world of Penn United Technologies, where machining is not high-tolerance work; it is rough work. The world in which Cabot lives is a more precise place than where the rest of the firearms industry resides.

The industry apart from Cabot starts with billet to produce a slide and frame. Cabot uses 4140, but not just any 4140. It specifies the purity. The company's experience has shown that the purity of the steel makes a huge difference, when it comes to the hardening process. You not only have to have billet of the proper purity, you have to verify it, every time.

This kind of detailed attention goes back to the philosophy that helps United

The Jones' cannot be kept up with.

The world in which Cabot lives is a more precise place than where the rest of the firearms industry resides.

The American Joe.

Penn serve other industries. You have to verify *everything*. From the material to the dimensions of the parts that you produce, everything has to be a known. That is the only way you can produce a 1911 that does not require a gunsmith for anything other than to assemble it.

It is totally unheard of, in the 1911 world, to not fit a part. The act of being a 1911 gunsmith is one largely of having the understanding and skill to put the parts together. Some people, like Stan Chen, make an art of it. Stan will spend an entire day working on a thumb safety, polishing, and fitting. He is, without question, a master gunsmith and a craftsman of unsurpassed skill and passion. There's no less passion and skill at Cabot, but the craftsmen there

do things differently. Look at it this way: If you could use technology to create a violin more amazing than a Stradivarius, would that diminish the original? I say that such is not the case, only that they are different.

In order to make a slide that does not require fitting, the dimensions on the frame are fit to five ten-thousands of an inch on each side of the frame rail. That dimension is not allowed to vary by more than two ten-thousands of an inch. Of course, at Cabot Guns they verify this, if you would like. They will use a Zeiss Prismo Super Accurate Coordinate Measuring Machine that is accurate to forty-millionths of an inch to measure your gun and generate a report. This Dimensional Analysis Tolerance Report is

pretty amazing. The one I saw shows the pistol in question exceeded the goal by one-third. Amazing. Truly amazing.

When you produce components that are that precise, you tend to get frustrated when you purchase parts from other people. One example of this is with barrels. Cabot made the decision to purchase barrel blanks and, being the company it is, the first thing its engineers did was measure them. Turns out some of the most highly thought of barrel producers do not, according to Cabot, produce a consistent product. So, what Cabot does is purchase a lot of barrels, measure them, and reject those that cannot be finished to the company's standards by way of some advanced grinding technology, to produce what it considers to be a

useable product. For those that are kept and ground on, Cabot tests each one, because, even from some very high-profile barrel makers, the accuracy varies. (As an aside, and before I continue, I know what you're thinking, and I thought the same thing: When it comes to accuracy, and all that fine parts fitting aside, is it the barrel or the ammunition? Of course, Cabot asked the same question, so its folks searched out and tested ammunition until they found the most accurate round that is commercially available. For them, and likely for you, Asym Precision Ammunition was found to be the most consistent on the market.)

There is a method of forming parts called Electric Discharge Machining. It is not unheard of for other firearm pro-

Bringing out the beauty of the steel was a goal when creating the National Standard.

NATIONAL
STANDARD

PENN UNITED TECHNOLOGIES
CABOT, PA
PENN003

The National Standard.

A National Standard mirror set.

ducers to use this method, though most use it to form rifling in the barrel. The advantage is that no stress or heat is produced to harm the temper of the barrel. It is a pretty amazing way to do things. You create a template from graphite and remove the metal at a particle level under fluid via electrical discharge. You can produce shapes that cannot be created using other modalities. Of course, at Penn United, the EDM department is but one of the specialized divisions.

It may sound as though all this technology is like a futuristic fantasy whereby no human hand is ever dirtied. But even

the most advanced grinding techniques on the most state of the art equipment requires an experienced operator. It is not as though you chuck up the part and hit a button, then go have a cup of coffee while you're checking Facebook and waiting for the machine to do its thing. The talent and experience of the operator is *critical*. From what I am told, the most important sense that any machinist can have, and the high-tech machinists at Penn United are no exception, is their ears. Apparently, you can hear whether a certain tolerance is achievable and when it has been achieved. Of course, the fin-

ished product is then verified, but an experienced operator can make a huge difference; the very fact that the Cabot 1911 takes no fitting is proof of the gun's precision, just as it is the machinists and craftsmen who made it so.

Remember that I told you the entire 1911 project started out as a morale booster, so the craftsmen there have fun. For instance, someone got the idea to make a true Damascus slide. Unlike other pistols that use powdered Damascus, Cabot used traditional methods, folding the steel. More than 50 layers of stainless steel are fused by Chad Nichols, Da-

mascus craftsman extraordinaire. When asked, Cabot's CEO and founder Rob Bianchin said that if they had known what a pain it was, the unique gun might never have been produced.

Another example. At the NRA Annual Meetings in Pittsburg, a man at the Cabot booth said, "No one will make me a left-handed gun." After some thought, Rob brought up the idea in a meeting. The room got silent. Everyone was thinking about how to do it and, when they created the SouthPaw, they went so far as to rifle the barrel in the other direction. It is a *true* left-handed gun. In addition

True mirrored guns - even the rifling is reversed.

Deluxe 1911 Mirror set.

to being cool and useful for the left-handed shooter, the SouthPaw also gave the Cabot folks the opportunity to make some neat gun sets. High-end collectors always like sets of guns, but to have a Southpaw and a right-handed gun is totally unique.

The Cabot guys enjoy playing with guns as an art form. They have a set of pistols with Obama on the left-handed gun and George W. Bush on the right. There's also a set with Ted Nugent on the right and Piers Morgan on the left.

One thing you will notice about the guns of Cabot's is their amazing finish. The company employs master polishers who spend hours upon hours shining up guns.

"The first time I saw one, I thought it was still wet from the blueing tank. I didn't know that a gun could look that way," said Bianchin.

There is no school for this kind of work, only apprenticing with another master polisher. I understand that it takes years, five or six, to become so skilled. There are no wheels or automation. The polishers work with diamond compounds and stones under a microscope.

"We have two full-time polishers that are among the best in the world," Rob said. "Our guns have gotten a lot of attention and a lot of people have gotten credit, but I don't think our polishers get enough recognition. They work in the shadows, but are key to our 1911s being so beautiful."

Beautiful they are. And the most precise 1911s made. An unparalleled achievement.

I bet that raised moral.

A Damascus slide is the only imported component at Republic Forge.

CHAPTER

5

REPUBLIC FORGE: THE ALL-AMERICAN MAKER

THERE IS NOTHING MORE AMERICAN than the 1911. Nothing. Not apple pie, not baseball, not even the Colt Peacemaker. And of those all-American 1911s, there is no 1911 that is more American than that of Republic Forge.

A newcomer on the block, the company's tag line is, "World Class 1911 Pistols. Made by Americans, For the Republic." I am here to tell you, the folks there mean it.

Benny Deal is a businessman with a wide variety of experience. His inspiration to start a 1911 company was homegrown and reflected his values. He started with the location, chosing the sleepy little town of Kerrington, Texas, which is about a hundred miles northeast of Amarillo, which is a nice way to say, "nowhere." With less than 10,000 people, and not a dozen traffic signals, Benny wasn't looking for nightlife, what he was trying to find was a place where a bible and a gun were uncontroversial and where his American values were shared. He bought three acres outside of town and started assembling a team while constructing a building. He also started purchasing equipment.

One of the most difficult things was finding manufacturing equipment that was built in America. This was important to him, so he took a lot of time making it happen. Apparently, there are, for instance, only two companies that build drill presses here in America. The rest are made in China, Taiwan, and places like that. Even the basic workbench was an issue, but Benny finally found a suitable woodworking

bench that would do the job.

Like virtually all manufacturers of 1911s, Republic Forge has to rely upon parts. With that cropped up another issue. While the parts company may have an American name, it's often and usual that they source their parts from all over the world. So, despite the label, the part may have been produced in Loas, Pakistan, Korea—you just don't know. After months of researching, Deal and his team finally were able to find all-American parts suppliers. In order to ensure a supply, Benny keeps a large inventory.

When asked about MIM (metal injected molding) parts, he said, flatly, "No." He explained that MIM is neither really fish nor fowl. It isn't really metal at all, rather, it's metal fused together with a binder. As you can tell, he isn't a guy who's going to compromise in order to save a buck. Cheaper though they might be, "good enough" is not good enough.

Are there any parts that are not American-made? Yes. Republic has a beautiful Damascus slide that it sources from Sweden. It is the only place in the world Benny says he is aware where he can buy them. So, if you are a Damascus 1911 slide producer in America, you might want to give him a call.

Of course, this is a book about guns. All of this is for naught if the guns are not good. To make sure that was the way it should be, Benny found a master gunsmith in Jeff Meister. With more than 30 years' experience with the 1911, he is a true craftsman.

The mindset for the company is not only "American" and "quality," but also "durable." If you look at its website (more on that later) you will notice that all the guns are Cerakoted. It is tough, wears well, and is available in a lot of colors, so it is easy to customize a gun for the customer. While Benny loves the look of a blued gun, it is just not as durable as Cerakote. Too, while the company may dabble in other finishes, until it is surpassed, Cerakote is the finish of choice at Republic forge.

Such a wonderful finish matches the gun. Republic Forge makes a quality, no-compromise 1911. And that is not just talking about the gun itself, but also the values of the company that makes it.

CHAPTER

6

FROM STI
IS BORN SVI

VIRGIL TRIPP IS A GUNSMITH and machinist. He is also a bit of a mad scientist. Whether it is karting, cycling, or shooting, when Virgil focuses his high-powered brain to the problem, some interesting solutions emerge.

It was about 1990, and Virgil was about as busy as he wanted to be. He was building race guns for USPSA (United States Practical Shooting Association) competitors. It was a heady time, and there were no rules stopping innovation. The race to create the fastest shooting gun with the highest capacity and the least amount of muzzle flip had turned into a full-scale war.

Virgil wasn't the first one to think of creating a modular 1911. He may not even have been the first one to design one. What he was, for sure, was the leader in creating one that was commercially viable.

The process started by bringing in Sandy Strayer. You see, while Virgil can machine anything, he did not have the knowledge to do the complex plastic molding required to create the gun that would become known as the 2011.

Working together, Sandy and Virgil created a design and got a patent. They also became partners and created the company Strayer Tripp Incorporated. Both their names were on the patent, which wasn't an issue, until things started going bad between them. The reasons and the blame for that break-up vary, depending upon whose version you believe, but in the greater scheme of things, they matter not.

What does matter is that, in a rather public divorce, Sandy Strayer left STI and, along with Michael Voigt, started his own company, SVI, an obvious play on STI, and began building 2011s of a similar, modular design.

Since SVI started in 1994, things have changed. Voigt is no longer there, and Sandy's son, Brandon, runs the shop. Other shifts include the fact that the frames are now machined from billet. There's is also a true custom gun, unlike the production method of most other companies, including S.T.I.

Marketed as Infinity Firearms, SVIs are highly prized, and there is no place more so than in the 3-Gun and USPSA worlds. Brandon Strayer says, "We had very great success with our six-inch limited pistols. From a standpoint of balance and sight recovery, as well as additional velocity, which allowed the shooter to reduce their powder charge, but still make power factor."

The problem is that the six-inch pistol doesn't fit in the IPSC box. Like most of the shooting games, IPSC has a literal box of certain dimensions in which each gun must fit. Where others saw the box as being a limiting factor, SVI saw opportunity.

"We developed our 5.4-inch pistol, do-

It may be a little grippy.

Diamond plate is not only cool on trucks. ing it in both a single-stack and a double-stack. We are totally within the rules of each division [Limited and Open]. The trick is to add barrel length and reduce the length of the beaver tail. We also reduced the length of our mag well with a flat section on the back, so as to maximize the length of the pistol at 225 millimeters." This increased barrel length is said to gain the shooter three or four power factor points over a Government-length gun. The increased sight radius and muzzle weight makes it a very user friendly gun.

Another SVI invention is the interchangeable breech face.

"It is not only manufacture-friendly for us, it is also shooter-friendly. Some of our guns might see 200,000 rounds through them. As the barrel wears, we can increase the size of the breech face, taking up the hood to breech face tolerance. As it wears, we continue to push the barrel forward, and the pistol will maintain that original lock up and accuracy."

This design can also be used to make a multiple-caliber gun.

"Prior to the interchangeable breech face, you had to have a gun for each caliber. Now, a lot of our guns are shot by competitors internationally, and in Germany, for instance, one can only own eight pistols. To have an inexpensive way to shoot multiple calibers from the same handgun can be a major advantage for a competitor in one of these countries.

Brandon is also quite proud of the modular trigger. In addition to looking cool, the SVI trigger allows the shooter to change the face of the unit without disassembling the gun.

"With the interlocking trigger system, there are seven inserts to choose from, both curved and flat and of various lengths."

Titanium is a gummy material to machine, and many people don't like to do it. Apparently, Brandon has no such compunction. He says there is nothing that the right tool will not handle. Besides, whatever issues there are with it, SVI thinks it's worth it.

"A client had an aluminum frame, high-capacity .45 that weighed 30 ounces unloaded. We built him a 26-ounce pistol, .45 ACP, complete titanium. In addition to decreasing the weight of the gun by a quarter-pound, we increased the ammunition capacity."

SVI does something else pretty interesting.

"On our titanium and aluminum frame pistols, we do a tool steel rail insert that runs the length of the slide," Brandon explained. "You get back to the slide-to-frame fit exactly as an all-steel pistol would have.

"Right now, I'm building a full titanium Steel Challenge pistol, which would work fine for Multi-Gun, too. Draw speed and quick transitions are going to be a breeze. With lighter power factory ammunitions, you don't need weight in the pistol to counteract recoil—rimfire recoil out of an Open-class pistol that is ultra-light. That is a huge advantage for a competitor."

A few years back, they brought the production of the barrel in house.

"Wil Schuemann was a brilliant mind,

when it came to the physics of actually what's going on as a projectile goes through the barrel. Schucmann Barrels helped us develop our manufacturing. We start with 416 rifle barrel steel and then test them. We have a testing fixture that totally takes the human out of the equation. Even with cast lead projectiles, we were getting 1.6-inch groups at 50 yards."

The excitement is apparent, when Brandon talks about the future of SVI.

"We're done with the modular frame and grip, but what's the next greatest idea? What is going to push the envelope further, make the competition stand back, be that next patent?"

I predict that it is that drive, that push towards the future that will keep SVI on the cutting edge for years to come.

Simple elegance.

CHAPTER 7

LUKE VOLKMANN: DELVING INTO THE DETAILS

THERE ARE SOME PRETTY AMAZING CRAFTSMEN out there, and there is no doubt that Luke Volkmann is one of them. When you see his guns, even those of the "working" variety, you see an attention to detail that is uncommon, to say the least. As to his fancy-schmancy guns, well, they might be equaled, but none surpass.

Of course, looking good is nice, but it's also useless if the thing that's beautiful doesn't run. After all, being broken down is no more fun in a Ferrari than in an Edsel, hell, maybe less so because of the price.

Luke knows how to make a gun work. He was under the wing of none other than Ed Brown. Yes, *that* Ed Brown. While there, Ed Brown himself, as well as his son Wade, trained Luke in the fine art of 1911 gunsmithing.

It was during the time that Luke was there, from 2003 to 2007, that the fine guns of Ed Brown were discovered by the mainstream. Demand for them skyrocketed. Ed ramped up production; Luke's gunsmithing skills were needed, as well as his ability to train new employees. While he appreciated the opportunity to supervise, though, it was assembly line work.

By "assembly line," I do not mean to make it sound like they were building Model Ts. One skilled craftsman accomplishes one task, say, something like fitting a slide, then passes it off to the next work station where another skilled craftsman will do his work. There are some benefits to doing things this way. Some will argue that if all you do is fit sears all day, you get better at it than you would fitting sears while

Volkmann Centennial.

also trying to gain the skills to build the whole pistol. Most of the larger custom shops operate this way, and there's nothing wrong with that. But, if you are a perfectionist, and especially when you have the talents of Luke Volkmann, you want to do it all.

Striking out on his own, Luke found an investor, moved to Colorado, and started Volkmann Custom. No longer constrained by the lack of options offered at Brown, he began to personally construct, from start to finish, every gun for each and every client. Over the next three years, Luke built 200 guns and proclaimed they were "one masterpiece at a time."

It would be nice if I could tell you that this is a happily ever after story. Alas, it is not. The investor was a fellow named George Horne, and he wanted more. Of course, Luke, thanks to Ed Brown, was no stranger to training people and was willing to expand production, albeit his way; he was willing to mold a talented gunsmith into a master like himself. But George wanted an assembly line to boost production. Luke tried, but was unable to convince his partner that individual workmanship was the entire premise on which the company had been founded. Things came to a head, as George insisted they go to an assembly line process. Luke refused. In the end, despite

offering to buy him out, George stopped production and Luke had no choice but to quit his own company.

This was a difficult time for Luke. He was honor bound to take care of his clients, who had not only ordered guns, but also put down deposits. Unfortunately, George had the money. So, Luke couldn't refund any money, and now he didn't have the funds or facilities to build the guns.

It took a couple of months to get a plan together, but he contacted the clients his former company had left hanging and told them that he would honor their agreements, even though he had no idea if he would collect their deposits

back from his old partner (he never did.) Explaining that it would take a while, he would personally build their guns, if they could please be patient.

Working feverishly to create a new company, this time a sole proprietorship, Volkmann Precision began producing guns in 2011, which of course, screamed, "anniversary model." The first 10 pistols were dubbed Centennial Editions. They sported gold inlays, case colored frames, and classy engraving. While very pretty guns, they are not any more precise than any other Volkmann Precision 1911s— which is to say they are very precise.

Luke starts the process by talking directly to the customer. He gets a feel for

Old-school engraving makes for unsurpassed elegance.

Luke's idea of a "working gun."

how the gun is going to be used. They discuss the options, and he gives them a rough idea as to when he is going to deliver their gun.

Manufacturing begins with a 4140 forging that Luke cuts on a five-axis CNC machine. Most companies would be happy to have their frames within a few thousands of an inch, but that is not near good enough for Luke Volkmann. A half-thousandth is what he's looking for. He file fits parts by hand and then begins lapping; starting with 240 grit, he ends with 500.

This attention to detail is apparent in every aspect of the guns and their many options. One of those options is a Volkmann High Grip Cut, which is a

notch machined into the frame just under the trigger guard. I have to confess, this didn't look right to me on a custom 1911 of this quality and high finish. On a highly modified race gun, yes, anything goes, but most Volkmann Precisions pistols are classic and classy. I'm not saying that this notch is unattractive, but it is not something you see everyday on this pistol with which we are all so intimately familiar. When you feel it, however it feels good. It gives your middle finger a better reference point than it would otherwise have on an unmodified frame. Because of this, you get a more consistent grip. In addition, the slightly flattened spot seems to give you a firmer grip with less effort. Perhaps this is an

illusion, but it seems to work.

Another feature Luke will incorporate is a Volkman Gripwell. In this he reshapes the magazine well, not simply beveling it, like everyone does. He also incorporates the grips into the act, so that they are part of the bevel. In addition, there is a front-to-rear arc that helps funnel the magazine into the gun. It is an innovative solution to a problem that many before have tried to solve.

While it may sound as though everything is done by Luke, by hand, that is not the case. He may polish the frame to an amazingly smooth finish, but then Doug Turnbull does the case coloring. It's not just the frame that's case colored, either. Unless the customer speci-

fies otherwise, the grip safety also gets Turnbull's treatment, as do the mainspring house, the magazine catch, and the plunger tube. Yep, the whole lower part of the gun is case colored, giving it a unique look.

Luke is an Old World craftsman with modern tools. He starts with a state of the art mill that is computer numeric controlled, and he finishes with a half-inch square of sandpaper on the end of his finger, meticulously polishing. There are few people that have that ability, that drive, to delve that deep into the details. But Luke Volkmann is such a man, and his guns show it.

Centennial editions.

CHAPTER 8

BILL LAUGHRIDGE'S CYLINDER & SLIDE

(AND ALL THE OTHER IMPORTANT PARTS, TOO)

BILL LAUGHRIDGE IS AN INTERESTING GUY. If you ask some folks, he's famous for working on double-action Colt revolvers. If you ask another, he is one of the greatest Browning Hi-Power experts in the world. His Adventurer pistol may be the smallest 1911 produced. But, if you ask *him* what his claim to fame is, he will say it's his remaking of the Colt 1903 Pocket hammerless pistol in .45 ACP.

Of course, an original Colt 1903 Pocket Hammerless was not a 1911, although John Moses Browning's penchant for simplicity does mean that the two guns share some design elements. Bill's re-creation is, however, a 1911. But let us not get ahead of ourselves.

As a young man, Bill was fascinated with all handguns. Heck, he still is. When he was a young man in 1971, working in a machine shop, he used to hang out at a little sporting goods store on the weekends. The store did some repair work on the side. While Bill was there one day, the owner's son was attempting, and failing, to put a Colt Woodsman together.

"He was trying to force it, and it was obvious to me that he was going to break it. His father obviously thought the same thing and told him, forcefully, to stop. He then turned to me and asked if I could put it back together. I did it, and that's how I got my first gunsmithing job."

Bill established a good reputation soon enough; not only did he have a quick, mechanical mind to go with his interest, he truly loved the work. When another,

The Cylinder & Slide Trident model.

full-time gunsmithing job came along, he took it. At the time, the main competitor to his new employer had a huge backlog. So, when the shooting community discovered where Bill was working, he was quickly inundated with, literally, hundreds of firearms to work on.

It took a few years, five or so, before he set out on his own and Cylinder & Slide was born. By then it was 1978, and IPSC (International Pistol Shooting Confederation), was really starting to take off.

"Back then, the most exotic 1911 was one with a Swenson ambidextrous safety and an adjustable rear sight from a Smith K-frame," he told me.

It didn't stay that way for long. The arms race was soon to begin, and when it did Bill started steering his work towards self-defense and concealed carry guns.

"I love working on the exotic guns, but, for a while there, a race gun could become obsolete in 60 days. If you have a backlog, the gun you are building is outdated before you start. That isn't a way to create a happy customer."

It also was a time where the cost of shooting IPSC was driving some shooters away.

"We were seeing a lot of states starting to pass concealed carry. So, we drifted over to making more personal guns. Of course, we have always supported the law enforcement and military communities."

Today, Cylinder & Slide makes what is, perhaps, the smallest 1911.

"I'm pretty sure our 3.1 Adventurer model was the first true mini-.45 available that worked, and we're still building it today. The grip of it is about a half-inch shorter than an Officer's model."

Top: Perhaps the most compact 1911 in production. Bottom: C&S' Pathfinder model.

Of course, imitators followed.

"After a few years selling them, some companies started figuring out they could make a three-inch gun and finally figured out how to make it work, but nobody cuts the butt as short as we do. They're all afraid to—and probably rightly so. When people grab a .45 and their little finger goes under the magazine, they're scared, but, in all reality, the gun recoils straight back and you're right back on target. The recoil is not excessive. They are real popular with the deep carry guys.

"We really got rolling when a writer named Evan Marshal, who came by our tent at the Second Chance shoot, in Central Lake, Michigan. I had set up a bench and was working on a competitor's guns. Evan was looking around and took an interest in a Smith & Wesson 45 ACP that I'd built. It had a spare .45 Long Colt cylinder and a custom barrel. He wrote an article about it for *American Handgun*, and that really stoked the fire.

"I love all kinds of guns, but the trickier the better. Smith & Wesson revolvers are so simple to me, but the Colts were fascinating, because they are so much more difficult to work on." With a laugh, Bill added, "I still have a bag of parts from my first Python Adventure. I distinctly remember that a railroad detective from the Union Pacific Railroad had brought that gun in with a broken cylinder bolt. That's where I learned that Pythons were hand-fitted guns!

"I bet I have made every mistake in the world, because I'm pretty much self-taught. I was helped immensely by guys like Jim Clark, Sr., and Armand Swenson and Ron Powers. They really helped coach me through some stuff. Even Bob Chow was kind enough to help me over the phone on some things. I've been fortunate to have enlisted help from some real, old-time, great gunsmiths and pistolsmiths. They were truly wonderful guys"

Bill recalled a visit to the John Browning Museum, at Union Station, Utah. His friend, the writer Roy Huntington, had

A 1911 Anniversary model.

invited him on the trip and had set up a private viewing of some of Browning's prototypes. They included a hammerless .45 prototype, as well as a 1910 prototype. At one point, Bill couldn't contain himself.

"I said to the custodian, 'Do you mind if I take these apart and examine them? I will give them a good lubrication and everything before we put them back together, 'cause they're all in the white [unfinished].' The guy just said, 'Heck, if you can get them back together, I don't care.'"

Bill and Roy looked at each other, each wondering silently, *Are we really going to get to do this?* then set down to the task at hand.

The hammerless .45 has a large grip safety reminiscent of the pocket model. Bill describes the fire controls as also being very similar, although the takedown is totally different.

"It took a while to get it apart, because the slide stop didn't have a takedown notch and there's no bushing. Finally, we discovered that the entire breechblock, if you want to call it that, was separate from the slide. You could rotate the entire breech assembly and slide it out the back. Only then could you take the slide off, remove the slide stop, and take the barrel out."

Bill was ebullient, as he described the gun.

"It was just fabulous. Browning did things simply. I didn't think we're going to have any springs flying and that jazz, but we surely looked like two bomb squad guys taking apart a bomb. We were so afraid something was going to fly out."

Apparently it was, as one would anticipate from a Browning design, very straightforward. Still, Bill and Roy were worried.

"Let's just say, it was intense there for a while.

"I've been privileged to take apart the hammerless prototype and the 19 prototype. I've been through the 1900s, the 1902s, the 1903s, and the 1905s through the World War I guns and World War II guns, including many prototypes. The 1911 didn't just happen overnight. It was a long progression."

This of course, leads up to the recreation of the 1903 pocket Hammerless in .45 ACP. Bill always loved the Colt Pocket Hammerless guns. He has them in .32 ACP as well as .380 ACP. He is also a fan of the .45 ACP cartridge. At the time, he had not seen John Moses Browning's prototype, so he thought that his dream was only his.

Being an expert on the 1911, and the lines and proportions of the two being similar, Bill had planned on making a hammerless 1911, styling it like the 1903. The stumbling block was the internal extractor of the 1911. That wouldn't work on the 1903, since that gun is sealed on the rear. That all changed when Caspian started making slides with external extractors.

"That's all it took to fulfill the dream of creating a Pocket-style .45."

If you take a Commander slide and put the extension on an Officer's frame, you have proportions almost identical to the original Pocket models. As a matter of fact, the curves on the back of the gun are elongations of the original curvature. The result is, perhaps, the most beautiful and elegant 1911 ever made.

It's all kind of funny, because one of the most unique guns Cylinder & Slide ever produced didn't make such a big splash. Bill, student of historical guns that he is, recreated the original 1911. He has examined a half-dozen "pre-serial No. 500" guns. Between his measuring and photographing the original gun and acquiring a set of original blueprints, he discovered *all* the differences.

"There are more than 19 parts that have been changed since the original, some to make them stronger, others changed for ease of manufacture. But the brilliance is that they could be changed without modifying the pistol. You could use either the old or new part, and the gun would work."

What is Bill Laughridge's next project? With his intimate knowledge of 1911s, penchant for history, and love of all things handgun, who knows? Perhaps a recreation of a model 1910?

COLT: A FAILED SUICIDE ATTEMPT

Once the standard of the industry, Colt has repeatedly been on the brink of failure over the last 70 years. During the heady times of World War II, the company was running 24 hours a day, seven days a week. But despite the proceeds from large military contracts, Colt was almost bankrupt; management had arrogantly spent like the war would go on forever. As one can imagine, after the war to end all wars was over, the need for such weapons ceased overnight.

To say that Colt had spent the war contract money like a drunken sailor is an insult to seamen. The resulting lack of cash made it difficult to retain the skilled workforce when production ceased. It is important to remember that these almost 15,000 workers had maintained the highest rating for quality from the military. After such an amazing performance, they understandably were very angry, when Colt shut down production for almost two years and made little effort to keep on their workers until a new strategy could be put into place.

Colt somehow managed to muddle along until 1955, when they were acquired (officially a merger) with Penn-Texas. With some competent management and fresh money in hand, Colt was to meet a new and brilliant gun designer, Eugene Stoner.

At the time Penn-Texas was merging with Colt, Eugene Stoner was working on the M-16 and AR-15 for ArmaLite, a company created solely for the purpose of developing rifles with light materials, such as aluminum and plastic. The development of the gun and the military trials is a fascinating story, especially with regards to the infighting. For instance, John F. Kennedy's close friend and confidant, General "Max" Taylor, loathed the Stoner, while Robert McNamara, Secretary of Defense, was in favor of the design.

Colt, in a move that made the purchase of Manhattan for $24 look like the Indians were master negotiators, bought all the rights to the Stoner design for $75,000 and a small royalty. By 1963, Colt had received an order for 85,000 M-16s, the first order of many. This period of prosperity was good

for Colt bottom line, but did nothing for the ongoing issue that had plagued them for years: corporate arrogance.

In addition to mismanagement, Colt now had to deal with a union. Having made the error of giving the United Auto Workers a contract, the union, as is their nature, tried to suck the lifeblood out of Colt. In response to union demands, management began eliminating some of their most skilled craftsmen. While this didn't affect the M-16 or AR-15 significantly, it put a pinch on the quality of the 1911 and severely harmed the line of double-action revolvers.

By mid 1980s, the union had gone from work slow downs to out and out shoddy workmanship, before it finally decided to strike. January 25, 1986, is when the picketing started. For four long years, production was zero. Zero. None. De nada. The troubled company was, effectively, out of business, but the union and the State of Connecticut, purchased Colt. Of course they couldn't run it, and the revitalization effort was bankrupt in two years.

With new management finally, in 1996, Colt got a break. Awarded a government contract, the company finally had a little cash flow to stem the bleeding of red ink. It also did some dorky things like playing with "smart gun" technology and, many would say, turning its back on consumer sales. Double-action revolvers were discontinued.

By the turn of this century, Colt tried to regain a piece of the consumer market. Of course, the years of shoddy workmanship, political faux pauxs, and indifference to the public made it a tough road to hoe. That said, I am told that things have gotten better. While the 1911s that I have seen were of average fit and finish, I am told that the custom shop is doing some outstanding work. I cannot say this with any certainty, as it is nearly impossible to get information from Colt. Perhaps I am wrong, but it seems that despite all of the trips to the brink of dissolution, the corporate arrogance remains. Without a doubt, it's a very sad commentary on a company that once ruled the firearms world.

CHAPTER 9

NIGHTHAWK: THE RISE TO THE TOP

MARK STONE WASN'T A GUN guy. As a kid, he shot a few pistols, deer hunted a little, plinked now and then. Even now, he still isn't a guy who carries 24/7, and he doesn't have a giant gun collection or even more than a few guns for home protection. What Mark Stone is, is a businessman.

His business acumen led him to be a commercial loan officer at a bank. He owned a few businesses. He worked for Tyson Foods. He understands how to make things work.

Living in Arkansas, Wilson Combat is the 8,000-pound gorilla—well, who are we kidding, Wilson Combat is an 8,000-pound gorilla *everywhere*, but, in the little town of Berryville, Arkansas, with less than 5,000 residents, Bill Wilson's enterprise looms even larger.

Mark Stone went to church with a couple of guys who worked at Wilson Combat. After services one day, they approached him and expressed interest in going out on their own. With Mark's business expertise, banking background, and the fact that he owned some commercial buildings, they thought he might be the guy to put together a new company.

Mark thought about it very carefully. One of the fellows who'd approached him was one of the top sales guys at Wilson. The other two were gunsmiths, one relatively new, the other a very long-time Wilson employee.

Mark knew what he was up against, but, with these kinds of partners, it seemed

Fit and finish is job No. 1 at Nighthawk.

feasible. In order to be fair, they started out as equal partners with 25-percent ownership each. Of course, Mark's new partners had never run a business, at least not on this kind of scale. They knew what parts cost, but had no idea about the true cost of business. To them, it all looked easy and profitable.

So, with some talent and some knowledge they started: no guns, no parts, no suppliers, no equipment, no website, no customers—not even a name. They began to meet and strategize. They first came up with a name and started to figure out the different models they wanted to offer. That turned out to be many. The next challenge was figuring costs, which varies greatly, depending on volume. The fixed costs are just that, of course,

fixed, so, with them, it doesn't matter if you build 50 guns or five. They also had supply problems; no one knew who this new company Nighthawk was. Besides, many vendors didn't want to anger Wilson Combat. Most of the fledgling company's early vendors had them paying C.O.D., which led to an early money crunch.

Les Baer is another savvy businessman. He saw the potential in Mark and his partners and was happy to sell to them. Interestingly enough, the first Nighthawk pistols had Les Baer slides and frames. In fact, the very early ones said "Les Baer" on them.

The BATFE says that the frame is the "gun" and it requires a "variance" in order to put a name on it other than the

one that is on the license of that gun. So, if, for instance, Kimber were to be contracted to make a frame, the company buying it could file paperwork that says it is okay for them to etch the name of the buyer into the frame, but it also has to have the address of the company that manufactured it. Les Baer got a variance for this, and the next run of Nighthawk pistols were stamped, appropriately, "Nighthawk, Hillsdale, Illinois."

While the wait seemed interminable, it is truly incredible that the first Nighthawk pistols were shipped in August of 2004. With early money problems, Mark needed and was able to secure another loan, and they were also able to get a vendor to start manufacturing their own slides and frames. While these were

steps in the right direction, Nighthawk still didn't have any real control of its manufacturing process.

Mark Stone says about the early parts, "Sometimes you wondered if they weren't sending us the stuff that *they* couldn't sell to anyone else. The dimensions were all over the board, so we put extra man-hours into each gun. That is expensive and time consuming hand fitting."

Other problems came up because of the partnership. More Wilson people came over, until they had four owners and four employees. That made for a difficult "Chief to Indian" ratio. Mark was still working for Tyson Foods, too, and would come to Nighthawk to do the books before heading for his full-time

The T3 line of pistols is ideal for concealed carry.

The weight on the muzzle never actually touches the slide of the Predator.

The Predator barrel adds weight, reducing muzzle flip.

job. He and one of his partners were also the only salesmen. It was a challenging time, to say the least. They would make a call to a vendor and say, "This is Mark Stone from Nighthawk Custom," and the potential buyer would start the conversation by saying, "Who?" Not exactly the beginning of a promising sales call.

The partners at Nighthawk knew that if they wanted to compete with the big custom names like Wilson Combat, Les Baer, and Ed Brown, they had to make something better and cheaper. Otherwise, why would the customer switch from a known, high-quality product with which they were already familiar? As Mark explained, "We really had to lay it out there, offer better customer service, a better warrantee. Today, we of-fer not only a lifetime warrantee, but we pay for shipping both ways."

The partners kept on building rela-tionships and working on improving their product. They continued to grow, albeit slowly. They improved relation-ships with some vendors and, as they decided whom to purchase from, they didn't just look at price. They wanted to become true partners with their ven-dors. They also wanted to receive the best quality parts. Not only did this lead to good relationships, but it saved mon-ey. Mark estimated that a pistol being returned cost $300 at the minimum and up to $500 at the top. In addition to the loss of confidence by the customer, it is expensive, so, building the best pistol is smart business all around.

As Nighthawk distilled its processes, it then began to develop more and more of their own parts. This helped the company improve its quality. It also started getting away from cast parts; the leg would break off a safety or tiny hammer cracks would develop.

"Sometimes you would be prepping a frame for more than three hours, and it's looking beautiful, and on that last sanding stroke a big pit opens up," Mark explained. This led Nighthawk to making the decision of having all of its parts machined from bar stock. Every. Single. Part. I do not know of another manufacturer building a totally machined 1911. This is something that Mark is very proud of.

"We have a great relationship with a vendor right here in Berryville, which does an outstanding job for us. With every part being a fully machined part, we are not only building the best gun we can, it is almost eliminating warrantee work."

Nighthawk is also about trying to be important to the local economy and community.

"Our frames are from forgings machined right here in Berryville, Arkansas, by an outstanding company."

Of particular importance to the company is for folks to know that Nighthawk never used MIM parts in their guns.

"Some MIM in the non-stressed parts may be fine, but there is a perception that MIM isn't good. That's probably not right, because, like anything, there's a wide variety of quality. Still, our goal from the beginning was to build the *best* 1911 on the market. You don't do that by saving money on a part that 'will do.' You put in the best quality part you can produce and you hand fit it."

YAMIL SUED PHOTOS

This is outstanding fit and finish.

Nighthawk Signature series. While Nighthawk was finally on firm financial footing and producing some outstanding guns, the income was not what some were looking for; over the next few years, the company lost two of the partners. By 2013, Mark had bought out the last partner, thereby becoming the sole owner of Nighthawk Custom. In hindsight, this was to be expected.

Another issue that Nighthawk faced was hiring quality gunsmiths. They might have 200 applicants for a job, but the people who truly have talent might be one or two. Sometimes there were none. With this in mind, Nighthawk pays its people well above the industry standard.

"We have these super talented guys and we have to keep them. They are vital to producing great guns."

At this point, Nighthawk's quality was second to none, but Mark was always looking for ways to improve. In 2011, the company made the decision to go to a "one gun, one gunsmith" manufacturing model.

Like most companies, Nighthawk had one guy doing slide fits, one guy doing barrel fits, one guy doing barrel rolls, triggers—you get the idea. While it can be argued that if all you do is trigger jobs or safeties, you do that job better, Mark believes, and I agree, that while it is gratifying to be a great magazine well blender, the single task doesn't stand up to the satisfaction of building a great gun.

"We had these super talented guys, so we asked ourselves, 'How do we get the most of their talent into the gun? And how do we get them to enjoy their job the most?' Being a gun builder has to be more satisfying than being a bobtail installer.

Nighthawk Enforcer.

YAMIL SUED PHOTO

Nighthawk Enforcer. "It took us a year to get everyone trained and our production to go flat. It was very expensive, but it was worth it. One gunsmith does it all. They pull the parts and do the slide-to-frame fit, the barrel fit, bushing fit, extractor, the trigger, safety—everything." With obvious pride, Mark continued, "They do it all, even going from dummy loads and slow feeding to taking it to the test range. They know what the Nighthawk standard is and they all have their own standards, which are at least as high."

It is an expensive process, which is why most companies, in fact virtually all sizable 1911 producers, use the assembly line method. Heck, even some of the tiny producers do so. For instance, Ben and Aaron Hayes, of Hayes Custom, has been fitting the frame to the slide and the barrel to the frame, with Aaron doing the rest of the work. Of course, when the term "assembly line" is used, it is not like tossing together a Model T. There are some great guns manufactured in this fashion. But Mark Stone isn't trying to produce just a great gun. He wants Nighthawk to be the best.

"If we can inspire these super talented guys to use all of their abilities, we will have achieved our goal. What better way to inspire these guys? They can produce a gun with their initials on it, and their great-great-grandchildren can say that their great-great-granddaddy built that amazing gun."

Since Nighthawk has gone to the "one man, one gun" production method, the reaction from the marketplace has been excellent. Unlike most companies who

YAMIL SUED PHOTOS

charge you a premium for such work—and usually a *large* premium—Nighthawk doesn't. Mark truly believes that quality people want to be remembered for something great, not for being a part of something great.

"Our people love it when a customer pulls a 1911 out of a Nighthawk bag and says, "Travis Gregory built that pistol. That is the best 1911 I have ever seen!""

Now they have people calling and asking for a specific gunsmith to build their gun. No upcharge, no hassle. Just a handmade, true custom gun.

The quality of Nighthawk Custom's 1911s has led to some pretty heady partnerships. Richard Heinie, one of the most respected names associated with the 1911, has partnered with Nighthawk. The Heinie Series is produced to Rich-

ard's exact specifications. Chris Costa, world-renowned weapons and tactics trainer, also has a line of pistols made by Nighthawk Custom.

"Chris has been using our guns for years now, and it is, quite frankly, a privilege to be associated with him. We want to produce the finest fighting 1911 ever made."

The partnership that is truly outstanding is that with Bob Marvel. Recognizing the path that Nighthawk Custom was on, Bob saw an opportunity to expand the use of his unique recoil system. The Nighthawk/Marvel Everlast Recoil System is said to go more than 10,000 rounds before a spring change is necessary, and it dramatically reduces felt recoil and muzzle flip.

Now understand, Bob Marvel pro-

duces his own guns. This is unlike other people with whom Nighthawk has partnered with, like Richard Heinie, who has sadly quit production of his amazing 1911s, and Chris Costas, who is a shooter, not a manufacturer. The partnership with Bob Marvel is truly unique. Late in 2011, Bob himself travelled to Berryville, Arkansas, and trained one of Nighthawk's master gunsmiths to produce the Bob Marvel Custom model. It took months of training and planning before the results were perfect. Needless to say, they didn't send this gun writer a Bob Marvel-edition Nighthawk. Those are only built special order, and the waiting list is very long.

It has been a long road for Nighthawk Custom. In the beginning, it struggled to survive. There were many incarnations of its 1911s and more issues than the owners would like to remember. It was Mark Stone's persistence and business savvy that pulled the company not only through the hard times, but also to the top of the quality mountain.

In writing this book, I have learned a lot of the inner workings of dozens of 1911 manufacturers, as well as that of many vendors who supply 1911 parts. I have seen all aspects of the business, and I must say that Nighthawk is, perhaps, the most impressive.

Quite frankly, when I started the research on Nighthawk Custom I expected that they were just another "parts assembler." There's nothing wrong with that, of course. I've shot some great guns from companies that don't manufacture a single part. But, with Nighthawk, what I discovered was a man committed to quality in producing the finest 1911 on the market.

So, is Nighthawk Custom producing the finest 1911 on the market?

It just might be.

ON BEING HUMBLE

When I was writing this book, I went out of my way to ask people who are familiar with the subject to double-check my facts, in the name of accuracy. Mark Stone looked at the rough draft of this chapter and verified that it is factually correct, but he strongly disagreed with him being the focus of the Nighthawk story.

You see Mark is a humble man, and he says that he is only one of many who created Nighthawk and made it what it became. He would argue that there are dozens of people who deserve recognition. He is also a man of great faith, and he would also say that all the glory is for God, not for Mark Stone.

My thought is that there would be no Nighthawk, were it not for Mark. He was the glue, the consistent force that kept it together through the hard times. With apologies to Mark, is my opinion that there is no other way to tell the story of the company.

An Ed Brown Special Forces.

CHAPTER 10

ED BROWN: IT'S PERSONAL

ANYTIME YOU SEE A MAN'S name on the side of a gun, you know that it is personal. There is a pride, a satisfaction, and a responsibility, when that name is yours. Since the name Ed Brown is associated by some of the finest 1911s on the market, it is obvious that he takes his reputation very seriously.

Like many in the 1911 community, Ed Brown started out as a shooter. Remember, back in the 1960s, bullseye was the game. At the time, Ed was a member of the Missouri National Guard and, like all military units, it paid high attention to its shooting teams, it was quite an accomplishment to even make the team. Ed Brown not only made the team, he worked his way to the rank of Master.

Ed has the mind of a machinist. If you have ever been around such folks, you understand that their minds work differently. They are like engineers, but more practical. They don't think about if something can be done, they think about the ways to accomplish it. So, as Ed was working on his own pistols, accurizing them wasn't the challenge that it would be for others.

That understanding of things mechanical came naturally to Ed. His father was a machinist and had a small shop in his basement. The sound of a lathe and the smell of cutting oil were early memories for Ed. While it may seem inconceivable now, Ed remembers running the lathe when he was 10 years old. Bite that OSHA!

In 1967, with his shooting career doing well and his understanding of metal

An Ed Brown Kobra Carry.

and all things mechanical in place, gunsmithing became an easy sideline. Anyone who has spent time in a gun shop knows that it's a lot of work and there is no glamor. Still, Ed put in long hours working on shotguns, installing recoil pads and other simple, bread and butter projects. He did good work, and a local shop started using him to outsource its gunsmithing services. That company later became Graf & Sons, an outstanding company in the reloading community.

Since Ed had started a family, his one-man shop wasn't enough to ensure the financial success he desired, so, when he was offered a job at a machine shop, he simply had no choice. He would work all day at the tool and die company and work nights and weekends gunsmithing. One would think this would be a detour from his path to becoming one of the premier 1911 producers, but such is not the case. The experience he gained pulling double duty was integral to that end—but I digress.

His talent and intelligence, as well as the fact that he was a perfectionist, made Ed's star rise quickly. Different manufacturing companies clamored to hire him to create tools and dies. His outside work led him to many prestigious operations that included, but were

An Ed Brown Executive Carry.

An Ed Brown Executive Target

not limited to, Kodak, General Electric, Chrysler, and Homelite, as well as Ford and General Motors.

As Ed expanded his gun shop, the first piece of equipment he bought was a lathe. This allowed him to not only start making parts, something that he would do for the rest of his career, but also perform barrel work.

A bit of trivia for any of you tool geeks out there, the lathe he bought was from what was then called Clausing Manufacturing Company, now known as Claus-ing Industrial. That company has always been known for producing some of the finest lathes in the industry. Is that interesting? Well, quite frankly, no. But it does seem to be a bit of an omen that Clausing Manufacturing Company was established in the year 1911.

With a growing family, a growing business, and his services being in high demand from the manufacturing industry, it was time to move. This is when Ed ended up in Perry, Missouri. His first actual shop might be humble by today's

An Ed Brown Classic Custom Stainless.

An Ed Brown Special Forces.

standards, but the 24x40-foot shop was a pure luxury to Ed. The year was 1979.

By now, Ed had embraced the new sport of practical shooting. He was a regular on the IPSC (International Practical Shooting Confederation) circuit. He wasn't just competing; he was running with the big dogs. Chip McCormick, Mike Dalton, Bill Wilson, Mickey Fowler, and others were his competition.

With his perfectionist nature, he was soon climbing the ranks. Now rated Master, he was garnering national attention. A fifth place finish in the Bianchi Cup is quite an accomplishment—he was no longer just "the local guy that did good." His personally modified Colt Gold Cup became an object of desire.

Not unlike the Jim Clark, a friend, mentor, and advisor, Ed's success at the range helped him expand his business. He would go to a match, compete, impress a lot of participants who thought it was the gun that made the difference, and get him to do work for them. When he was going to a match, he would have pistols to deliver to customers. When he left the match, he invariably had a carload of guns he was taking back to his shop for repair or customization. Shooting was more than fun, it was business.

Another nice boost to business came when Ed forged a friendship with Ray Chapman. For those of you unaware of who Ray Chapman was, let me tell you, he was one of the giants of PistolCraft. A contemporary of Jeff Cooper, he studied and experimented with shooting methods. The "Chapman stance" is a modified Weaver stance, and, while these days, most competitors use the isosceles, the Chapman is still a very efficient and effective platform. Not only was he an innovator, Chapman was a world

An Ed Brown Signature Edition.

champion shooter, an innovator, and an instructor. His friend and colleague Jeff Cooper dedicated his book *Cooper on Handguns* to, among others, Ray Chapman. In addition, he referred to Ray as "the Maestro." Impressing Jeff Cooper wasn't an easy thing to do, but Ray did so.

Ray would not allow anyone except Ed Brown to work on his 1911s. At Ray's school, the Chapman Academy, when a

An Ed Brown Special Forces Carry.

student's gun would have a failure, Ray would call Ed. Even after a long day at work, the student would have their repaired gun back before the next day of class. This wasn't only good for business, since people were flying in from across the world to attend Ray's shooting school, this was also good for Ed Brown's reputation.

By the early 1980s, Ed Brown was being pulled in a lot of directions. He was asked to use his machining, engineering and software knowledge to evaluate a new tool. This tool is one that we take for granted today, the CAD-CAM system (computer aided design-computer aided manufacturing.) It was an arduous project, and he spent dozens of weeks working on it. Just the programming took four months, while working with the winner of the project, McDonald Douglas. Even with his lack of range time during this period, he still did very well competing. Ed came in ninth in the USPSA championship (United States Practical Shooting Association, the American arm of IPSC), and fifteenth in the IPSC Championship. Add a sixth in another the Bianchi Cup, and one has to conclude that he was at the top of his shooting game.

Eventually, Ed finally realized he couldn't do it all. Running his gun business, his engineering work, and shooting competitively was just too much. Something had to give. So, in 1984, he reluctantly gave up shooting.

Of course, Ed is not the kind of guy to let grass grow under his feet. Even though two full-time jobs and a family with young kids would be enough to overwhelm most people, to Ed, this was "found time." With his newfound schedule he started inventing. One of his innovations was the Maxi-Comp, perhaps the

most elegant compensator ever made. It was shaped exactly like the front of the slide and, in fact, had the front sight affixed to it. It stayed in place, with two oblong ports on the top, and the slide worked behind it. Not only was it, for its day, a darned good compensator, but the weight being so far forward was great at holding down the muzzle, reducing "flip."

He also started producing the Maxi-Well, a magazine well integrated with the mainspring housing. While we see them all the time today, Ed was the inventor. His beavertail grip safety was also soon invented and produced. You see, Ed Brown had learned from the late, great Armand Swenson. The "old man" recognized that you could only build so many pistols, but you could make an infinite number of parts.

The parts business was thriving. By 1988, Ed quit working for the tool and die company and was working full time to expand his gun business. He immediately bought a CNC mill and started making parts. By 1994, the company now known as Ed Brown Products was bursting at the seams. Ed built a 5,000-square foot building and started adding more equipment—but not just any equipment, automated equipment.

While he is not at liberty to reveal who they are, a large number of 1911 producers use Ed Brown parts, the reason being that his parts are second to none, when it comes to exact tolerances and consistency. These days Ed has three machine centers that are totally automated, running 24 hours a day, seven days a week.

Most men would have stopped there, but Ed Brown, perfectionist, wasn't done. He would not stop until he pro-

An Ed Brown Executive.

duced his own 1911. Sure, it's business, but it is also reverence. Ed believes "The 1911 remains, to this day, the finest fighting handgun the world has ever known."

In 1999, Ed started producing frames, and the goal of producing the finest 1911 was one step closer. It wasn't long before the entire gun was being made by skilled craftsmen, with Ed Brown's name right on the side. He has never been a "this is good enough" kind of fellow, and his guns show it. The fit and finish are outstanding, and the pistols shoot amazingly well. One thing you will not find, however, as you peruse his website, is an accuracy statement. Ed tested all quality barrels that were available, trying to determine whose was the best. What he discovered was that the .45 ACP is only so accurate—and his guns are more accurate that the ammunition. With this in mind, he guarantees that his 1911s will extract 100% of the accuracy that the ammunition is capable of.

With his manufacturing background, Ed is an assembly line person. He believes that a man that, say, fits slides all day gets to be an expert at it. He has different stations of skilled gunsmiths focusing on one or two aspects of the build process. These days, his son Wade supervises the gunsmiths and makes sure that the guns are to his father's exacting standards.

So, where is Ed Brown today? He is in semi-retirement, in the office only three days a week. He works on some research and development projects, helps plan for the future of the business with his other son, Travis. I am sure he looks back with pride at some of his accomplishments, like the 1991 Pistolsmith of the Year award from the American Pistolsmith Guild, developing the Snappy

An Ed Brown Kobra.

camera for Kodak, creating the software for the 1994 Corvette throttle body and the early General Motor's cruise control units. Perhaps he even smiles thinking about how he changed the firearms industry by developing the now ubiquitous beavertail grip safety or the bobtailed 1911. I imagine he also looks at his company with pride. After all, it is supplying the industry with some of the finest parts available. But the thing that he is surely the most proud of are his guns, outstanding 1911s that say "Custom by Ed Brown," right on the slide.

CHAPTER 11

WILSON COMBAT: ONCE REMOVED FROM JOHN MOSES

BILL WILSON IS LINKED TO THE 1911 in a way surpassed only by John Moses Browning himself. In addition to being a world champion 1911 shooter, one of the longtime leaders of 1911 development, and producer of some of the finest examples of the gun, he has also promoted the shooting sports that feature, you guessed it, the 1911.

Yes, I know that I am a heretic for mentioning a mere mortal in the same sentence as (trumpets blare as the clouds part and a beam of golden light shines at the mention of His name) John Moses Browning. Okay, I am a heretic, but the facts support me.

Bill's father was a watchmaker and was expected to follow in the trade. In addition to growing up in the business, he went to Oklahoma State University's Institute of Technology, one of the country's finest watchmaking colleges. While one might think that watchmaking and guns have little to do with one another, being able to manufacture a part for a watch makes gun work look rudimentary. Referring to the gun, Bill told me, "The parts looks so big and the tolerances so large, it was not much of a challenge."

He grew up in Berryville, Arkansas, so the fact that he is a country boy is a trait come by honestly. Like nearly everyone who grew up in such an environment, he had always loved guns. Going to college didn't change that. Working in the family business, he decided to start a gun shop on the side. He had no way of knowing that small shop was the first step to building an empire, but I digress.

Bill loved to shoot and, after scraping up enough money to buy a Colt Python, he began shooting PPC (Police Pistol Combat) shooting. As the name implies, it was primarily a tool for training police officers to shoot more effectively. Much like the International Defensive Pistol Association is today, PPC required participants to fire from behind barricades that simulated cover. As time went on, participants realized that it really wasn't training, but actually more a game, and the equipment wars began. It wasn't long before bull barrels and impractical sights and ghost holsters ruled the day.

Even competing with a relatively stock revolver, Bill did extremely well. He became a PPC Master, even without any of the tricks of the gamers. Then, like most competitive people, once the spot was mastered, he became bored and began looking for something new. Bill had heard about a club in Missouri, which had "combat" matches. Once he shot the match, the die was cast—and he needed a 1911.

His first gun was a stock government model and it was, predictably, not what

Bill Wilson, 1982.

he needed. Unreliable, inaccurate, and slow, he sent it off to a famous gunsmith (who will remain nameless). The watchmaker was unimpressed with the work. Not only was the gun not improved, function had suffered as a result of the "custom work." He tried another big-name shop and, again, was disappointed with the results. He sold it off and bought a bone-stock Colt Gold Cup.

Bill says that the Gold Cup was a great gun and looks wistful when he speaks of it; along the way, he sold it off. But it was a great gun, reliable, and did everything he needed it to do. Still, like a golfer who thinks a new set of clubs will make a big difference, Bill looked to equipment to elevate his game.

Bill was unintimidated by the 1911. After all, the parts were not only big, but enormous compared to the watches he was trained to repair. In addition, the tolerances were comparatively loose. He decided he could do better.

There were very few manufacturers of custom parts back then. The first place he looked to was none other than Armand Swenson, the genius gunsmith that was an early pioneer in combat 1911s. He also ordered some parts from Arnold "Al" Capone of King's Gunworks. The first Wilson Combat was born.

Bill started competing with his new gun and, as expected, did extremely well. It wasn't long before fellow competitors were asking him to build guns for them. Eerily, like Jim Clark, whose bulls-eye success led him into the gunsmithing business, Bill soon had a thriving side business.

The jump to becoming a full-time gunsmith was not a leap that Bill took lightly. He had been expected to take over the family business, and his father

At the 1983 World Championships.

was none too happy at an otherwise decision. Besides, he didn't have the financial reserves to start a new business. One thing that you can say about Bill Wilson is that he is not a timid man. Against all odds, he jumped in with both feet. It was touch and go for a while. He was a one-man shop for about a year, but then hired another gunsmith to help him. Still strained but growing, it took a couple years, but he had more work than he could handle.

The fact that Bill was a great shooter was something that is not to be overlooked. While he was shooting and winning, his stock was rising. This gave credence to his products, be them guns, parts, or accessories. After all, when the guy is holding the trophy, his name is one that is to be respected. Another thing Bill did from the very beginning, was to get his products into the hands of gun writers. If you were writing an article, a column, or a book, Bill would do his best to help you. This book is a great example of that. When I asked Bill for background information, the first thing he did was invite me to his ranch. We went over the details of his company, his shooting career, and his guns. There has been no question that he has not answered, although some he has asked not be printed. No call, text, or e-mail has gone unanswered. That type of open, honest relationship with writers got Bill some nice, well-deserved press.

If you ask him, Bill is quick to credit Armand Swenson and Jim Clark for his

Interesting shooting positions are sometimes required.

success. They both knew what he was going through and were glad to help. Bill had clients from across the world sending him their guns for him to modify. But Bill wasn't going to be satisfied until he had a gun with his name on it. He started purchasing guns and modifying them to his standards. Within a few years, he was contracting to get components, and that was when Wilson Combat was truly born. He wasn't done yet, though. The next step was to make the entire gun on premise. Bill is very close to totally controlling every part that is manufactured for his guns, including barrels.

Another accessory, one that is most essential to the dependability of a 1911, the magazine, is a staple of the shooting industry. Some would argue that Wilson's are the finest on the market. I can only think of one other whose magazines compare.

Bill recognized that you can work on only so many pistols, but you can sell countless accessories. It was in the first few years in business that he started making parts. That was definitely a lesson he learned from Armand Swenson. In fact, one of the first Wilson Combat accessories was the "shock buff" invented by Swenson. Originally made of leather, eventually Armand discovered what the plastic highway cones were made of was ideal. Customers would steal traffic cones and drop them off so that they would be assured of getting their parts. The lot next to the shop had so many stolen traffic cones that Bill mentioned, only half kidding, to his nephew, John Jardine, "If the highway department ever comes by, we are going to jail!"

One day Bill Wilson was in his shop and asked if he could make those shock buffs to sell. Armand said something to the effect of, "Please, I wish you would. I'm tired of punching out those damned things."

The fact that Bill started making 1911 parts early on was truly one of the keys to his success. The parts business was underserved, and he was determined to do his best to change that. It is hard to imagine it now, but it wasn't that long ago that there were virtually no parts available for the 1911.

At the 1979 Second Chance match.

Of course, now Wilson has a full line of accessories. I dare say there is not a single part for a 1911 you cannot buy from Wilson Combat, most with more than one variant. Not only are Wilson's parts known for being very precise and reliable, if you do have a problem, the parts are quickly replaced. I have used many Wilson parts—extractors, mag wells, recoil strings—and I have never had a failure.

Wilson Combat magazines are, argu-

ably, the best on the market. The reason is simple: Constant development, constant tweaking, and outstanding quality control inspections. To this day, Wilson Combat is working on improving its magazines. It is unlikely there is another company that has such an existing, well-established product and that is still spending as much time as well as research and development resources to continue to improve.

Many have suggested that you cannot get compact 1911s to run reliably, but Bill Wilson has proven that it is not true. "The main thing you have to do to make any 1911 run reliably is to tune the timing of the gun. This is no different with a compact, although it can be a little more challenging." Yes, it can, but not for Bill. He says that in order for your compact 1911 to run reliably, you have to do two things: slow down the slide and lighten the ammunition stack.

You slow down the slide with a heavier recoil spring, and you also use a heavier hammer spring. There is another innovation that came out of his shop, and that is to use a square-bottomed firing pin stop. By lowering the point at which the firing pin stop comes into contact with the hammer, the slide has less leverage to push against the hammer. It's a small but brilliant innovation.

As far as the ammunition stack, it's all about weight. A full magazine loaded with 230-grain .45ACP is too heavy for the spring to reliably lift the round into place quickly enough. That is why Bill says not to use a projectile that is heavier than 185-grains in such compacts. Of course, using +P ammunition is unwise in a compact. Bill also says that .40 S&W roundshave the same problems, so the same rules apply. The proof is in the pudding, as they say, and Wilson Combat Compacts are the most reliable on the market. In fact, they are the guns that have changed the minds of many who have professed a compact will never run reliably.

Bill has had some great ideas that he never pursued. One is that he created a prototype of a pivoting trigger for the 1911. While not a new idea, the Ballester Molina was an Argentinian 1911 clone that was licensed by Colt back in the late 1930s. Colt's engineers supervised the

original production. This seemed like a great idea, and Bill decided to create a modern version of it. I'm not sure why he didn't pursue it, perhaps it was along the lines of "if it ain't broke, don't fix it," but it never got past the initial phase.

One thing that you can say about Bill Wilson is that he has never forgotten where he came from. He remembers the assistance men like Jim Clark, Sr., and Armand Swenson gave him. When shooting phenomenon Chip McCormick popped onto the scene, he also became an acquaintance. Chip was one of the fastest guys on the IPSC circuit, Bill Wilson was one of the most accurate. When Chip decided to use his fame to get into the gun business, he had Bill Wilson and Wilson Combat to look up to. Over the years, they have become fast friends and would both be happy to help the other. There are not too many owners of competing companies who would treat one another that way.

One thing that you can say about Wilson Combat is that, if it sees a market it can compete in, it does so. The company is, and with good reason, known for its outstanding 1911s, as well as its parts and accessories, especially magazines.

Wilson Combat also manufactures a full line of first-class AR rifles, everything from 7.62x40 WT (the "WT" stands for Wilson Tactical, and yes, it is a Wilson cartridge) to .458 SOCOM, a round that Bill personally loves for hog hunting. And let us not forget the shotgun line, Scattergun Technologies. In addition, Wilson Combat is also now working on

Bill doesn't just love 1911s.

and creating accessories for the Berretta 92 and 96 pistols. Bill has great admiration for those guns and has an extensive collection of them. I noticed that, on his website, he admits that going into Berretta work was partially "an economic reason to do some of the cool stuff that I wanted."

That said, do not believe for a second that Wilson Combat has lost its focus. That sleepy little town of Berryville, Arkansas, is home to the largest custom 1911 shop in the world. I do not know who second is, but they are far behind. At this writing, Bill employs almost 50 highly skilled gunsmiths. Interestingly enough, few of those gunsmiths have any gunsmithing school training. Over the years, Bill has learned that it is best to take a good old country boy with a good work ethic and a mechanical mind and train him.

"We start them off doing test firing, and then we move them to finishing. As their skill level increases, we move them to doing simple gunsmithing tasks. We have some guys that started out knowing virtually nothing who are now outstanding 1911 gunsmiths."

It makes sense. After all, who knows more about building custom 1911s than Wilson Combat.

Of course, the story is not about Bill Wilson and his company, it is about his guns. I decided to try out a Wilson Combat and see if the lore had weight. Is the king of 1911s crown deserved, or is it running on advertising and reputation? There was no way to know except to try one out, so I called up the company to order one. When I went to decide which model to order, I took the advice of Bill Wilson himself. You see, Bill competes with and carries a compact 1911. The

reasoning for this is he finds that, with the shorter sight radius, the rear sight is easier to pick up. This is especially true as our eyes age. In addition, the shorter, lighter gun handles more quickly, so target transitions are improved. Bill is not only a great businessman, but a world-class shooter, so who was I to argue? I ordered a Compact CQB in 9mm.

The first thing you will note is that this gun is a "bonny lass." Right out of the box it feels great. The 30 lines per inch checkering are about right, and the Wilson "starburst" grips not only look cool, they give a positive grip without

Wilson Pinnacle, the finest one yet.

Bill takes the "combat" part of his company's name very seriously.

Wilson CQB.

being too abrasive.

I took the untested pistol to an IDPA match. Yes, I know, that's a big no-no. One should always function test a pistol as well as make sure it works properly with your competition gear. I don't always follow my own advice. Sue me.

My first stage ended up being the best I had shot in a quite a while. Bill was right about the short sight radius. It is easier and faster to pick up the sights. It took a couple stages to really make friends with the gun, but, eventually, friends we became. It is a fast-handling, straight shooting gun and my scores improved. All in all, it is a great gun for IDPA. Sure, I had to fend off my friends teasing me for using "a back-up gun" to compete, and, no, I didn't knock anyone off the leader board, but it is not the fault of the pistol. After all, I am no Bill Wilson.

It is not only me who liked the little gun. My daughter was teaching a young man to shoot handguns. She'd started him with a .22, but it was not long before he graduated to the Wilson. The small size and smooth operation had his groups shrinking in no time. I also let a friend shoot some of the 1911s that I have on hand, and, when he was done, he said "When you die can I have the Wilson?" I declined, if for no other reason for fear that he might speed up the process.

It is unlikely anyone could have predicted that the young watchmaker would end up with his name synonymous with the 1911 in a way only exceeded by that of John Browning himself. From the beginning, Bill Wilson was driven to be the best. The company that bears his name has an unsurpassed reputation and I am here to report that it is well deserved.

A Kimber Gold Match.

CHAPTER 12

KIMBER:
SAVED BY THE 1911

COUNTLESS COMPANIES HAVE BEEN CREATED to produce 1911s. Even more have been created to make parts and accessories for the 1911. But how many have been saved by the 1911? I can only think of one: Kimber.

Jack Warne knew guns. He had founded SportCo, after World War II. Many of the guns he produced were inexpensive trainers for the British Army, be they .22 Long Rifle, .22 Hornet, or a variation of the British .303. They were known for being very accurate, yet very basic guns. It was not long after he sold the company that Jack and his son moved to America. They wanted to produce a quality bolt-action .22 to fill the void left in the market, when Winchester had quit making the Model 52. Jack and his son, Greg, created Kimber of Oregon.

Their first gun was an outstanding bolt-action .22 Long Rifle, the Kimber Model 84. In addition to being very accurate, it was beautiful. Interestingly enough, that was not the original plan. Before production was started, Jack took a prototype of his rifle on a rockchuck hunt with some industry friends. Like his SportCo guns, the original Kimber was fairly plain. His friends convinced him the gun was special enough to put a nice stock on it. It was Leonard Brownell who designed the first stock, and with it, the timeless, elegant Model 84 was born.

Jack's friends had been right, appearance matters. Even though the rifle's stock pushed the gun into a higher price category than originally planned, initial sales were strong. This initial success led to expansion, not only of the product line, but with the addition of a second manufacturing plant. This put the company on financial thin ice, and it began seeking outside investors. The subsequent infusion of cash helped, but with it came more problems. It wasn't long before the Warnes sold their stock, and ownership was taken over by Bruce Engel, a timber baron. Being a force in the timber industry did not translate to success as a gun manufacturer. Add the near destruction of the timber industry because of the spotted owl lunacy, and

soon Kimber of Oregon was no more. Bankrupt and insolvent, the assets were sold off.

Almost immediately, Greg Warne decided to start another company, one also using the Kimber name. Partnering with Leslie Edelman, owner of Nationwide Sports Distributors, Kimber of America was founded. As it is with all new ventures, there were issues. Quite frankly, that history gets a little cloudy, but the bottom line is that Les Edelman ended up in control; the reason he was interested in Kimber was that, as owner of a huge gun wholesaler, he wanted an

An Ultra **CDPII.**

exclusive product to market.

In addition to production of the fine .22, Edelman had Kimber sporterize Mausers. The ship was finally headed in the right direction. But "steady as she goes" is not Les' way; he's more of a "full speed ahead" kinda guy. About this time, Chip McCormick was looking to Jericho Precision Manufacturing to produce 1911 parts. Discussions between Chip and Les ensued, and the idea morphed into producing the whole 1911. Edelman invested in Jericho, with the idea of producing a precision handgun.

It's important to remember what was going on in the firearms world at this time. There were no well-made production 1911s on the market. Colt was trying to put the wheels back on the bus. Springfield was making guns, but you didn't go to the range with a new one, you drove right past the range

to your favorite gunsmith. Of course you could buy a Wilson, Bear, Brown or one of many other custom guns, but they came at a high price and long wait.

Chip McCormick, world champion shooter and 1911 expert, was brought in to consult on Les' new endeavor. He and his engineer, David Locke, demanded that all the components be machined to, at that time, unheard of tolerances. The resulting gun was to become the finest production 1911 on the market. In doing so, Kimber had created a new category: the precision production 1911.

The stars had aligned to not only keep Kimber alive but thriving. That in itself is nothing short of miraculous, but the drama wasn't over. Sadly, Kimber fell victim to a man that Federal Judge Legrome Davis described as the "… most specially talented liars that I have ever met in my life." Denis Shusterman had convinced Les Edelman to appoint him chief

A pair of Kimbers.

financial officer of both Nationwide Sports Distributors and Kimber of America. Like all good con men, Shusterman had ingratiated himself in every important way; the most important was that Edelman thought that Denis was his friend. Little did Les know that both his companies were being fleeced. Meanwhile, Shusterman was living a lavish lifestyle as though he would never be caught. The FBI was investigating another embezzlement case and came across Shusterman's crimes. With a "go big or go home attitude," the con man had bought a $2 million home in California. He also, inexplicably financed some movies, including a couple of teen slasher films. Busy guy that he was, prosecutors said he had at least three, if not five mistresses. With most of the $10.8 million he garnered coming from Kimber, the impact was huge, even with the success that Kimber was enjoying.

Les Edlerman might have thought the name of one of Shusterman's films, "The Demon Within," was autobiographical, but his faith in Kimber never wavered. He kept plowing money back in and kept the ship right. Production never waned. The casual observer would never know that anything was wrong.

So where is Kimber now? I decided to find out.

Kimber makes a wide variety of 1911s, at least one for what I imagine is every conceivable purpose. I counted 84 models on its website. They include, but are not limited to, the Pro Carry II, CPDII, Ultra Carry II, Ultra CPD II, Ultra TLEII, Compact CPDII, Pro CPDII, and the Custom CPDII. While I find the model names incomprehensible, it is a fact that my face broke into a wide smile when I opened the case sent to me and saw the Ultra Plus CPD II.

This Kimber is certainly a pretty little gun. All the edges are softened with a full "melt-down" treatment. The theory is that there are no sharp edges to catch on clothing while drawing. The only thing I have ever caught is the hammer, but even if it is just cosmetic, it is attractive. The black frame contrasts nicely with the brushed stainless accents. The skeletonized match trigger is also brushed stainless, as are the beavertail, safety, and slide. Wooden grips give a nice organic contrast. While I can't tell one wood from the next, they are reported to be rosewood. Not only do they have a nice, old-school diamond pattern, but a lovely, deep, rich color.

Meprolight Tritium three-dot sights sit atop the short slide. When I say short, I mean short. The whole thing is under six inches. The aluminum frame keeps it light, too. Without a

A trio of Kimbers.

YAMIL SUED PHOTOS

**Warrior SOC
with a Crimson
Trace laser sight.**

magazine, it weighs only 23.9 ounces.

The little gun points like you would expect: perfectly. The familiar grip angle and short sight radius makes it very quick-on-target. Being .45 ACP, even with the full-length grip it, this seems like a "carry a lot, shoot it seldom" kind of gun—exactly what you don't want to do with a carry gun.

You can learn a lot from a dirty gun, so I ran over to a local indoor range and got it hot. I brought 200 rounds of the dirtiest, Eastern Bloc, steel case ammo that I had on hand. First off, the gun has recoil. Nothing that is unmanageable, but being so short and light, it twists in the hand, making follow-up shots a little slow without "muscling" the gun. Still, it is an accurate little bugger. At 21 yards, the ubiquitous "ragged hole" appeared two inches to the left of the bullseye.

That particular range I was on that day doesn't allow rapid fire, but the safety officer was lenient. She looked the other way while I did double taps and some triples. It takes some concentration to control the recoil, but the full-size grip made it doable. According to the shot timer on my iPhone, at seven yards I could put three into the two-inch square in about .6-second, fairly consistently. No doubt Bruce Piatt would laugh at those splits, but hey, I'm no Bruce Piatt. I could fire it faster, but accuracy suffered.

I could not find any witness marks on ejection, but I did notice that the nose of the round was hitting well down onto the frame. Of course this is a function of the magazine, not the gun. Still, even with at least one questionable magazine, it ran flawlessly.

Getting a compact auto to run is no easy trick. The light slide needs to be slowed down enough to allow the magazine to lift the next round into place. One of the biggest mistakes people make with a compact 1911 is to run too hot or too heavy ammunition. While I am not suggesting this is okay to do, I used 230 grain +P as an experiment, and even with a less than perfect grip

,I couldn't make it jam. Again, I would never suggest you trust a compact 1911 .45 with heavy, powerful ammunition. Please note that I loaded it with 185-grain Hornady FTX Critical Defense for the trip home.

Reluctantly removing the rosewood panels, I replaced them with Crimson Trace Master Series Laser Grips. Installation was simple. Put the batteries in, add a "dust shield" (a thin layer of plastic between the grips and the frame) and screw them on. Sighting them on the wall, I adjusted the laser to be above the front sight by a couple inches. In addition to being a great sighting tool, it is a great training tool. It is also cool that playing with the cat becomes "training." (It should need no admonishment, but I'll give one anyway: Dry-fire training means no ammo in the gun, no ammo even in the same room in which you are training. Seriously. None. At all.)

One thing that I have learned over the years is that you don't truly know a gun until you run it hard. With this in mind, I hauled the Ultra Plus CPD II to a local IDPA club match put on by Mike Webb of Texas Tactical. Before you think me insane, remember that Bill Wilson competes with a compact. He believes that the shorter sight radius makes it easier when your eyes are not as youthful as they once were. Now, my eyes are not all that bad, but my arms have become too short.

When I arrived at the range, my friends almost immediately started making fun of me. Apparently they did not believe an aluminum frame compact .45 ACP to be a "competitive advantage." In an attempt to defend myself, I mentioned that Bill Wilson competed

with a compact and I explained why, but they were quick to point out that I am no Bill Wilson. They went on to say that I might not be qualified to carry his range bag. These are my friends. I need no enemies.

Despite all the support from my *amigos*, I was excited to run the gun. Being quick on target was an advantage. Long shots weren't a problem. Trigger is fine. I would have preferred a high visibility front sight, but the Meprolights worked fine. While I admit that I started slow, I was muscling the gun, trying to control the recoil. After a couple stages I got more comfortable with the gun and it was running pretty well. Although the lead dogs weren't worried about me catching them, my times were inching into the top 10. It was about then I had a failure to extract on a second shot in a string. A trip to the safe-table revealed nothing amiss. The extractor looked good and was nice and clean. At first I was pretty disappointed and was planning to call Kimber first thing Monday morning. Then I realized I was breaking a cardinal rule of keeping a compact running, a rule I preach like an evangelist at a roadside revival. In my haste to run out of the door, I tossed some "blaster ammo," Winchester white box 230-grain, into my range bag. The ammo-stack in the full magazine was simply too heavy. It was totally my fault, not the gun. One should never use ammunition with bullets heavier than 200 grains in a compact. When I realized my error, I reloaded the Hornady FTX Critical Defense, turned on the Crimson Trace laser grips, and confidently put it back in my holster for the ride home. This little dog will run.

YAMIL SUED PHOTOS

PART III

THE 1911'S SHOOTING STARS

CHAPTER 13

THE GAMES WE PLAY

F MY SOURCES ARE CORRECT, the shooting sports, as we know them today, had their genesis in Big Bear Lake, California. Legend has it that none other than Colonel Jeff Cooper himself organized fast-draw competitions. What started as a simple "who can clear leather fastest" game quickly turned into a game where different scenarios and stages were set up. The year was 1956.

It took a while until policemen, looking for ways to hone their skills, created "police pistol combat shooting" which, as the name implies, mostly had policemen competing. Soon, though, civilians began to pick up the sport. It was an era when the revolver ruled, but some 1911s made for combat began to make their way into the fray. The amazing Armand Swenson's guns were used. So were Jim Hoag's customized guns. Arnold Capone also had some guns that were modified for the sport. But the extended magazine releases, ambidextrous safeties, beveled magazine wells, all the things that we take for granted today, were fairly exotic at the time. The squared trigger guard, which Swenson favored, became a popular modification.

Four years after its introduction, PPC did not have a wide following. For all intents and purposes, this was the only game in town, but, even then, there weren't a lot of towns where they set up matches. A group of frustrated gun enthusiasts led by, you guessed it, Jeff Cooper, got together in Columbia Missouri and had a meeting. The result was the formation of the International Practical Shooting Confederation. This was a welcome change in the competitive shooting community, as there were finally a set of standard rules and a governing body to administer them, and thus was

born the modern sport of action shooting. The year was 1976.

Of course, when a bunch of highly competitive people get together, they look for every advantage they can get. The holsters started getting crazy—and impractical. Weights were hung off of the dust covers. Muzzle breaks or compensators, which directed the expanding gasses upwards to help control muzzle flip, became standard. In fact, the highly modified "pin guns," which were designed by Jim Clark for shooting bowling pins as fast as possible in tournament play, were used in IPSC.

The modifications and customizations increased over the years as the sport gained in popularity, and the highly customized 1911 became more commonplace among the serious competitors. The "arms race" continued, and advances in 1911 development were at full tilt. Smaller, faster bullets would make Major power factor and have less recoil than a traditional .45 ACP gun. Rob Leatham won the 1984 championship with a 1911 chambered in .38 Super. I addition to reduce recoil, the hotter load cycled faster and, most importantly, it enabled a higher capacity, so Rob had fewer reloads.

In the beginning, during the leather-slap, fast-draw competitions, the competitors were "point shooters." It is a technique in which no sights are used. That was the method of the day until Jack Weaver, Los Angeles Sheriff Deputy, started winning consistently. In fact, Jack's success caused Jeff Cooper to rethink his methods. It was Cooper who dubbed it the "Weaver Stance." Largely due to Cooper's wide influence, the Weaver Stance ruled the day. And why not? It is an efficient way to get a sight picture. Of course, IPSC competitors want to shoot fast and accurately, so they would use the Weaver and get an acceptable sight picture before they cranked off the round. By the 1980s, traditional sights had become obsolete, with the introduction of the dot sight.

The dot or red dot sight looks like a small optical scope, but inside there is a bright dot that can be adjusted to the point of impact for the bullet. Aimpoint had developed the concept in the 1970s, and, by the '80s, it was fully accepted and widespread use of the units had began.

The best thing about this type of aiming device is that both eyes can remain open. This is great for this kind of shooting sport, as you can use your full peripheral vision to pick up the next target. Sure the old timers hated them, but they hated the muzzle brakes, .38 Supers, and other advances in gaming, too, so in the end it just gave them something else to complain about.

Of course, while running around a stage and shooting targets, capacity was and is a huge factor in success. The quickness of the reload is of paramount importance. In fact, in IPSC, there is a universal understanding that, if you are moving, you are loading. Still, some flat-footed reloads still had to take place, so more capacity was always a good thing. Gunsmiths started cutting the grips apart and adapting them to take "double stack" magazines. These magazines, being wider, allowed the cartridges to be offset rather than stacked one on top of another. These wide-bodied 1911s not only made for more capacity, but the added weight aided in follow-up shots by reducing recoil.

In 1985, Para-Ordnance (now Para-USA, owned by The Freedom Group) began producing high-capacity frames in kit form to the market. Gamers flocked to it. Traditionalists complained. Put another way, everything and everyone in the game was consistent. The Para-Ordnance frames were so popular the company soon began producing complete guns, sent to customizers to have all of the "good stuff" installed.

Around the same time, IPSC had grown in popularity to the point that a governing body just for the United States, needed to be established. In 1984, the United States Practical Pistol Association, USPSA, was formed.

In 1993, the Para was joined by a modular, high-capacity 1911 dubbed the 2011. Virgil Tripp, a brilliant gunsmith and engineer, brought in an engineer and CAD expert to work out the details, and STI was born. The frame was fiber-reinforced plastic. Since it was less bulky that the Para, it was the hot flavor of the day.

By now, the traditionalists were totally fed up. The sport had strayed too far from any "practical" shooting applications for their taste. Led by Bill Wilson, they got together and formed a new shooting sport, the International Defensive Pistol Association, or IDPA. The founders included Larry Vickers, Wault Taunch, Ken Hackathorn, and John Sayle, in addition to Bill Wilson. They came up with rules that were designed to keep the sport inexpensive and realistic. Many of the IPSC competitors loathed IDPA, because they felt that they were saddled with too many rules. No matter which camp you paid homage to, one thing was for certain: The 1911 played an important role in both shooting disciplines.

The International Practical Shooting Confederation and its American chapter, the United States Practical Shooting Association always had a close association with the 1911. From the beginning it was one of the most popular platforms on which competitors built their guns. Back in 1976, the 1911 was one of the few auto-loaders that had a thriving parts and accessory industry. It's hard to imagine that today. Seems like you have an amazing selection of parts for today's most popular guns; be they Glock, Springfield XD or Smith & Wesson M&P, you can buy every single part from several aftermarket companies. That simply wasn't the case when IPSC was founded, so the 1911 was the way to go. Of course, the reader of this book is most probably already in agreement with that statement, USPSA notwithstanding.

If you want to shoot your 1911 in IPSC/USPSA, they have two divisions in which you can enter. The first is Production. The idea in this division is that the guns to be used are stock, no customization allowed, no race guns allowed, and no matter what caliber you choose to launch downrange, your magazine is limited to 10 rounds. With a plethora of 10-round magazines, this is a great place to start in USPSA. Heck, even your regular holster will be fine. In fact, the skeletonized holsters aren't allowed in Production class; the trigger must be covered.

Of course the traditionalists, the purists, would encourage you to go to the Single Stack division and they would have a point. After all, Single Stack is the 1911 club: Stock 1911s, no red dots, and limited to eight-round magazines. In this division, there is a certain camaraderie that does not exist in other divisions. These players are the ones most likely to quote Chuck Taylor or Jeff Cooper.

YAMIL SUED PHOTOS

The Smiths are ready to play!

The Limited Division is not really about the gun, but the magazine. There is no magazine capacity limit here. If you can carry it, you can shoot it. This is where the 2011s and other wide-body guns come in. I know, I know, they are not technically 1911s, but they are 1911 designs. The rulers of this class are the guns of STI, and their large magazine capacity is the reason. The other major difference between this division and Production is the holster. The craziest, most exotic holsters you can imagine are allowed. Not anything that you would use anywhere but at a match, but they are fast!

Then we get to the Top Fuel dragsters of the sport. The unlimited hydroplanes. The "if you can dream it, you can shoot it" division. Of course, I am talking the Open division. Want a weighted muzzle brake? Sure. Want a red dot sight? Absolutely. Prefer a holographic sight? No problem. Lighten the slide? Sure? As near as I can tell, the only restriction is that the magazine cannot be longer than 171.25mm. Here STI's 2011s get some competition. Virgil Tripp's old partner from STI started his own company, SVI (Strayer Voight International). They shared the patent for the modular framed gun. Sandy Strayer wanted to build full custom guns, and he does. Marketed under the name Infinity, they are excellent. They are also pricy. Because of this, they are often relegated to the "cost is no object" folks; those folks tend to shoot Open.

Now let's take a look at the "other" side. Since its inception, the International Defensive Pistol Association has been very friendly to the 1911. Is it because Bill Wilson, champion shooter and manufacturer of some of the finest examples of the 1911 ever made was a founder of the organization? Possibly. But remember the reasoning behind IDPA. Its founders wanted to create a gun game that was more about the shooter and defensive shooting and less about the game and the gun.

The idea with IDPA is that, while a Texas Star target is fun to shoot, generally speaking, attackers don't cartwheel while attacking. Thus, the stages in IDPA are set up to be, well, more realistic. You might be sitting at a table and have to draw and shoot targets. Or move to another position and shoot from cover, then move to another position and shoot through a port. This mind-set flows through the whole sport. For example, a shooter is penalized if they drop a magazine with live ammunition. The theory is that you would always want to take your resources with you when the flag goes up. The same desire to be practical and replicate real life goes to the equipment. There are very few modifications allowed. No muzzle brake, no optics. The goal is to encourage the use of guns you would likely carry.

The 1911 division in IDPA is CDP, or Custom Defense Pistol. They should have called it the "1911 Class." The rules are pretty straightforward. Your gun must be a .45-caliber or larger projectile. The gun may only hold eight rounds. Sure, you can download your Springfield XD .45 to eight rounds, but let's face it, it's a 1911 division.

In keeping with their "no equipment races" policy, there are strict weight and size restrictions. No oversized controls are allowed, for instance. It really is a division for pretty darned stock-only guns.

Enhanced Service Pistol, or ESP, is the next class up, and some gun modifica-tions can be made. You can add magazine wells, for instance. This is a good division for a 9mm 1911, as the power factor is 125,000. Some people use their STIs in this class, although they have to download their magazines to 10 rounds. The reasoning behind this is that many states have legislated ridiculous 10-round limits, so this levels the playing field across the country for scoring.

Those are the main differences between IPSC and IDPA. The interesting thing is that there is a certain amount of animosity between the sports. In my experience, USPSA/IPSC shooters tend to be very vocal in their hatred of IDPA. Very vocal. That there is a sport that has rules that don't let you run around and shoot whatever you want seems to truly offend. The USPSA website even takes a dig at IDPA:

> *...Practical shooting is pure sport conducted with little or no thought of the self-defense aspect of firearms use. However, USPSA members are generally the most proficient shooters in the world as witnessed by their domination in the world of firearms competition.*

Take that I.D.P.A.!

IDPA shooters, of course, tend to think of USPSA/IPSC as just a game. They tend to have a pious attitude, as though their discipline is more realistic, and therefore better. The term "gamer" is often thrown around as both a playful insult and a direct dig at USPSA.

Which is better? Who cares? I love the run and gun nature of USPSA and I like the more thoughtful, strategic aspect of IDPA. But, as a 1911 shooter, it is easy to stay out of the fray; the same gun and

magazines are legal in both, as is all of your ancillary equipment. Shoot both and let them argue about silly crap.

Want a different game? Steel Challenge is a great sport and is very 1911 friendly. Not only is Limited Ten a good division for the 1911, the sport has a division named Single Stack 1911. Yes, Steel Challenge likes its 1911s.

Limited Ten is just what it seems like. It is a limited ammunition capacity division. While you can modify some of your controls, like extended magazine releases and slide stops, you can't use optics, compensators, ported barrels, and the other "race gun" stuff. Most of the competitors use single-stack guns, but you see some wide-bodies, too.

Single Stack 1911 is the traditionalist division. Only eight-round magazines are allowed in Major and 10-round magazines in Minor. The holsters must be standard street holsters, none of the skeletonized rigs like you'll see in the Open Division.

Of course, the Open Division is where the 2011s of Infinity and STI shine, and competitors can load them with as much ammunition as they want. There seems to be little restriction as to modifications. "Gas pedals" are common and everyone has a compensator and some type of optic. Red dots and holographic sights are the norm. The ultra-fast skeletonized holsters are also required, if one wants to be competitive.

One thing you will notice, when looking at the divisions of these different sports, is that there is a lot of potential crossover between them, with regards to the equipment. If you are a single-stack 1911 shooter, there is a place for you in any of these sports. Shoot a wide-body, no problem. All have a division where your gun and accessories will fit. Of course USPSA and Steel Challenge have the Open Divisions, which IDPA does not, but still, you can shoot that heavily modified gun on most any weekend.

Chip, before the isosceles
and the thumbs-forward grip

CHAPTER 14

CHIP McCORMICK: STARTING AT THE TOP

WE ALL KNOW ABOUT CHIP McCormick magazines, perhaps the most prolific in the aftermarket. What you may not know is just what other influence the man behind the magazines has had and currently holds in the 1911 industry.

Chip always loved guns. He was a rifle guy. He had subscriptions to firearm magazines such as *Guns* and *Guns & Ammo* from the time he was six years old. He loved the challenge of a long shot, how you could use a rifle to reach out to things distant. He would rather make one long shot than shoot a lot.

Hunting gave him a purpose, so hunt he did. As a teen, he began shooting at longer at longer distances, but always interested in one shot, one kill. Young lad that he was, he was an ethical hunter. He loved to make a perfect shot and drop his prey in that boneless way that only a perfect shot can do. The advertisements in the magazines made him want to reload. He loved studying ballistics and honed his accuracy. When he would take an animal, if possible, he would find the bullet and see how it had expanded.

One day, in 1980, Chip was at the range in Austin, Texas, sighting in a rifle. He heard some shooting down in one of the bays. Whoever was there was making a commotion, shooting fast. Curious, he asked the range officer what was going on. As chance would have it, a local IPSC club was holding a match. The range officer told Chip he should go check it out, so he wandered down.

Conventional wisdom of the time was to use the leverage of the trigger guard.

The gun culture being the friendly place that it is, the IPSC shooters went out of their way to welcome him. They asked him if he wanted to compete; it didn't take much for them to convince him to shoot the match. Of course, he didn't have a pistol or gear with him, so the others loaned him what he needed. They explained the rules, and a good time was had by all.

Chip returned the gear, thanked them for their generosity and tutelage, and prepared to go home. As he headed to his car to pack up his rifle, the other competitors yelled at him to come back, because scores were being announced. He waved them off and kept heading back to his car. The range officer asked, "Don't you want to see how you did?" Chip answered "Naw," because it was his first match and, besides, they had some very talented shooters there, two of whom were highly trained, including time at Gunsite, Jeff Cooper's shooting facility. Still the group kept waving him back, so, not wanting to be rude, he returned. When scores were posted, Chip had won the match.

Having had such a great time and having done so well, he returned for the next monthly match and won that one, too. The following match was the U.S. Nationals and one of the club shooters had a slot they offered Chip. While he was honored, he really didn't have the money to travel to the match. The club members were adamant that he go.

Texas had never even placed in the top 100 of Nationals. Now if you know Texans, you know that they are a competitive bunch. The members of the club saw Chip as their best chance to make the state look good, so damned if they didn't go to local gun shops and get sponsors. One paid for the hotel, another the airline ticket, so Chip was off to the 1981 U.S. Nationals.

In only his third IPSC match ever, he came in fourteenth. Not only was this quite an accomplishment for any shooter, let alone a newbie, it also qualified him to get into the shoot-off.

Young Chip McCormick was hooked. While he is not one to brag, he has some amazingly fast reflexes—scary fast. He is one of those shooters for which everything "slows down." Athletes like that are rare, and their ability to stay composed in the heat of competition is often uncanny.

As I said, Chip was fast—very fast. On the draw alone, he estimates he had a tenth of a second on his competition over the first shot. If you add that up over a match, it might be two and a half seconds, so he had a distinct advantage right out of the box.

While he was fast, he was also a student of history. He noted that the military liked to cycle fighter pilots in their late twenties.

"In World War II, a pilot was considered in physical decline by 27 or 28. I was loving shooting, but knew I couldn't spend a lot of time at the top of the game."

Yet he did spend his time at the top. In 1983, he went to his first World Speed Championship and came in second. For those who don't know, the event is officially the Steel Challenge World Speed Championship. It is *designed* for fast shooters. There are no foot faults or anything like that, it's just a stand and deliver event with time being aggregated over the eight stages. Mike Dalton and Mike Fichman created the World Speed Championship, because they recognized the shooting sports had the potential to also be great spectator sports. Based on speed and simple rules, anyone watching could understand what the computers were up to.

The World Speed Championship eventually became successful enough that the Steel Challenge Shooting Association was formed, in 1988. This provided the platform to establish consistent rules for clubs to follow, and it quickly became one of the most popular of the shooting sports. With that popularity came prize money, making it one of the most lucrative shooting sports, as well. In 2007, Mike Dalton and Mike Fichman sold the organization to the United States Practical Shooting Association (USPSA), and today it remains an extremely popular event.

Chip had no meteoric rise to the top. He started there and stayed there. Competing against legendary competitors like Rob Leatham, Nick Pruitt, Mikey Fowler, and Jerry Barnhart, Chip was always in the hunt. After his second place finish to Fowler at the 1983 match, everyone knew that he was on the leader board to stay.

Chip's agile mind started looking to

equipment to give him an advantage. After all, if you are fighting a fair fight, your tactics suck. He had some people go out of their way to help him with his equipment. One was the venerable Bill Rogers. Bill is the holster designer who put Safariland on the map with dozens of innovations that include the first retention holster, and his was the first company to use Kydex, a unique acrylic that's easily formed. In addition, Bill is a shooter of renown. A former FBI agent and police instructor, he has won many shooting competitions. He still operates the Rogers Shooting School. Bill saw a star in Chip McCormick and was eager to help him by designing him a holster that worked specifically for him. To this day, Chip is thankful for Bill's help and friendship in those early times. "I was a poor boy then, working on a shoestring budget. Without the help of Bill and others, I could not have competed," he told me.

A tight budget didn't stop him from looking for other competitive advantages. The .38 Super, for instance, was and is a very accurate round. In fact, if you were to ask 1911 experts what cartridge they would use to construct the most accurate 1911, the overwhelming response would be the .38 Super. Chip recognized that by pumping up the volume of the .38 Super, he could make Major power factor and still have a lighter recoiling gun. He could also have more rounds in the magazine and, thus, have fewer reloads compared to those shooting the .45 ACP. The problem was that he kept blowing up cases.

"The unsupported chamber was giving me fits. I was shooting a Devel Gammon, and it was a great gun, but the cases wouldn't hold together. Jim Clark, Sr.,

was very kind to me. He knew I couldn't afford much and was very kind when he went to bill me."

Clark built Chip a fully supported, integrated barrel, so that he could develop a load to make Major. While only one of many innovations to his credit, Chip says, "Being one of the first to use the .38 Super in competition is something I am quite proud of."

Chip credits other with helping him along the way. One example took place at the 1983 Steel Challenge. Chip was on fire, smoking the competition and enjoying a five second lead going into the last day. For those not totally in the know, five seconds is a huge amount of time. It is an eternity. To put things in perspective, Chip won his first World Speed Championship by .07-second.

With what should have been a sure victory, Chip finished the match with a penalty or two, knocking him down to ninth place. He was demoralized. Bill Blankenship took the opportunity to offer some advice. Now, when a man that has won five bullseye championships in a row decided to offer you advice, a smart man listens—and, if you haven't figured it out by now, Chip's a smart guy.

Where Chip had made his mistakes was in his 40-yard shots. He was amazingly fast close in, but his accuracy suffered. Being a champion bullseye shooter, accuracy, of course, is something Bill Blankenship knows about. He gave Chip some advice regarding his mindset on that stage, helped him get a healthy attitude about the longer shots.

"Bill told me, 'Look, Chip, you've got to get over the hurt and learn from your mistake.' That's when he explained how he prepared mentally for a stage and what his thoughts were while he's shoot-

Do not doubt Chip's quickness. This is him smoking the late, great Bob Mundon with a laser gun game at SHOT show. Notice that Bob doesn't appear to be having as good a time as Chip.

ing. Bill's advice truly changed my mental preparation. Because of Bill Blankenship, I became one of the top two or three fastest on that stage. I made that stage my friend, as opposed to my nemesis."

Bill Blankenship also gave Chip some other key advice. Chip asked Bill, "How in the hell do you hit a 50-yard bullseye one-handed?" With a smile, Bill answered, "The key to shooting accurately, no matter then range, is knowing when the hammer is going to drop. When I'm shooting bullseye, I'm not trying to hold the gun steady all the time. The objective is to have the sights on target when the gun is going to fire. It's about timing."

Chip absorbed that lesson.

"I took that concept of timing and applied it to speed shooting. What I learned to do was to start bringing pressure on the trigger and put the gun where I needed it to be when the gun discharged. That really sped me up."

Sped up indeed. In 1986, he won the World Speed Championship. In 1988, he repeated as champion. Chip was enjoying success and figured he should use that to launch into the 1911 business.

Chip MCCormick with a couple World Speed Championship trophies.

"I realized that the success I enjoyed could be used to support a product line. That's the year I started selling the magazines"

Chip's big break came when he acquired the patent for the Kelsey magazine follower. Charles Kelsey was, without question, an absolute genius. The follower was just one of his many innovations. But, for all his engineering brilliance, he was a horrible businessman. Chip describes him as a man ahead of his time. Sadly, he didn't know when to quit research and development and bring the product to market.

"In 1983, when I blew the five-second lead, I was shooting one of Kelsey's guns, a Devel Gammon. His guns were beautiful, they were accurate—simply put, they were perfection. People approached him after the match with checkbooks and cash, begging him to sell them some guns. He flat refused, said they weren't ready for the market."

Because of his lack of business acumen, Charles Kelsey's company Devel went bankrupt. With that collapse, the patent for his follower became available. What made that follower so unique is that, when coupled with a spring invented by Walter Wolff, it allowed an extra round in a standard magazine. The follower has a compressed spring action, thus making extra room in the magazine.

"The Kelsey follower had been offered

to other people I knew, but they didn't think it was worthwhile. I did," Chip told me. "I begged, borrowed, hocked, and sold everything I owned to be able to buy that patent."

It would prove to be one of the smartest business decisions that Chip ever made, which is saying a lot, considering his success. With his acquisition of Kelsey's follower, the Shooting Star magazine was born. Interestingly enough, Chip is such a humble guy he was reluctant to use his own name, so he used the "Shooting Star" until he was convinced his name would actually help business. Today, of course, Chip McCormick magazines are a staple in the 1911 community. In fact, many special operations units, both military and police, exclusively use McCormick magazines. No, you won't find any of them named; Chip refuses to market on the backs of men and women putting their lives on the line. He does not believe those warriors should be exploited. The farthest he will go is to state that his magazines are "combat tested" and that they are used by "tens of thousands of law enforcement and military." Chip did reveal to me a few of the hundreds of special operations units that use his magazines. It reads like a who's who of spec warriors. Let me put it another way: If you thought of them, they probably use McCormick magazines.

One of Chip's great mentors was Col. Charlie Beckwith. "Chargin' Charlie" was no nonsense, and a tougher man never lived. At least twice he was written off for dead, once having been shot in the abdomen with a .50-caliber round. Not much stopped Charlie. He went through Ranger school and joined the Special Forces. Due to his brilliance and unconventional thinking, he quickly rose through the ranks. He rewrote the book on specialized warfare and created Delta Force, the elite counter terrorism unit.

After he retired, he and Chip met through a family friend. Chip described himself as a nobody, but he and Charlie really hit it off. "He was one of the most significant influences in my life,"

Many, including law enforcement, military, and special operation units, believe McCormick makes the best, most reliable magazines.

Chip told me. Charlie taught Chip ethics, how to evaluate people and, for lack of a better term, be a man of honor. Chip recalled a conversation they'd had, telling me Charlie had said, "'Chip, the most valuable asset you will ever have is your integrity and your honor. If you will always treat it that way, it will serve you well throughout your life.' And boy was he right. His lessons permeate everything I do. I don't cut corners when making a part or putting a business deal together. It was such a blessing to have a man like that in my life."

Chip McCormick now has several companies, but, because of the tutelage of Charlie Beckwith, they remain shrouded in secrecy.

"Whether it's consulting, working with a military unit, or just identifying my OEM customers, it is up to them to reveal our relationship. I simply won't do it."

Chip doesn't even reveal the number of companies he owns. Between consulting and manufacturing, your guess is as good as mine.

One thing about Chip is that he is constantly observing. One of his early business influences was Bill Wilson.

"His advertising is excellent. He also has a great feel for how to position a product in the market. When I was setting up my business affairs, my benchmark was Wilson Combat."

Since the early days, when Bill and Chip competed with each other, they were friendly. Bill was always the more accurate shooter, while Chip was faster. As the years have passed, they have become fast friends. Competing in the same market, not only with 1911 parts, but AR-15 items, as well, they still talk openly. I think it's kind of cool that two of the people most significant to the development of the 1911 are pals.

That said, due to his discretion and integrity, I really can't tell you what effect Chip McCormick has had on the 1911 other than it has been significant. He has manufactured millions of 1911 parts, consulted with many 1911 companies, created a magazine company whose products are depended upon by thousands of customers spanning the realms of military, law enforcement, competitors, and civilians. He has invented and developed aspects of the 1911 in countless ways. I can't tell you the numbers, or relay to you the stats. But what I can tell you is that Chip McCormick is a good man.

BRUCE PIATT: DECADES OF WINNING WAYS

T HERE IS NO ARGUMENT THAT Bruce Piatt is one of the greatest shooters of our time. He came onto the national scene in 1985. Since then, his accomplishments are too numerous to list and they are *still* piling up. They include five Bianchi Cup Championships, five Soldier of Fortune wins, and 20 USPSA championships in the Law Enforcement Division. The list goes on and on and on.

Bruce's story and his association with John Moses Browning's masterpiece is long.

Bruce Piatt has lived, God help him, his whole life in New Jersey, just outside of New York City. It was 1973, he was about 12, when he began bugging his dad to shoot. They had firearms, but there wasn't a place to shoot in the city. Bruce's father did have a friend with a farm in upstate New York. Bruce was allowed to go work there and shoot. Piatt Senior also enrolled him in a National Rifle Association Small Bore Program. Bruce and 10 or so other student learned to shoot standing, sitting, kneeling, and prone. An old former Marine taught them the basics. Bruce and his classmates learned sight picture, trigger, and squeeze on Mossberg single-shot .22s. They would shoot from seven p.m. to nine at an indoor range, not too far from their houses. After that, men would come in and shoot bullseye. Bruce would stay and watch the targets through a spotting scope. It was a local league, and while the 1911 was well represented, they had a fair number of revolvers, too.

Bruce's father had some revolvers and a Luger, a war prize from World War II. He

NRA Understanding The NRA Classification System

Shooting Sports USA

VOL. 22 NO. 8 AUGUST 2009

30th NRA Bianchi Cup
Adds New
Production Division
For The Rest of Us

No stranger to the winners circle, Bruce wins Bianchi again.

also had a Colt Officer's Match, which Bruce wanted to borrow so that he could shoot bullseye, too. But the league was just for adults, and Bruce was relegated to watching.

Eventually, he was able to start shooting bullseye, and he did well. Then he got his driver's license. With the distractions of girls and cars, shooting fell to the wayside.

Bruce got out of high school and got a job. Later, becoming friends with a po-

lice officer, the shooting bug took hold again. At the advice of this officer, he bought a Browning BDA (Browning Double Action) in .380 and took it to range orientation required to attend action matches at the local club. Bruce told me, "Back then, you pretty much just had to shoot an El Presidente and you were good to go." (The "El Presidente" is a drill where there are three silhouette targets, one meter apart and 10 meters from the line. The shooter is facing away from the targets, hands in "surrender" position or clasped behind the back of the head. When the buzzer goes off, the shooter turns, draws, and fires two shots into each target, reloads, and shoots each target two more times. It was developed by Col. Jeff Cooper to measure a shooter's ability to draw, fire quickly, and reload.)

Bruce used the little BDA to compete for a while, but it eventually became obvious he needed a better gun. He saved his money and bought a Colt Gold Cup, his first 1911 of many. One day, while looking at the *American Rifleman*, he saw an article about the Bianchi Cup. He was looking at the course of fire and, in typical Bruce Piatt form, thought, *I can do that!*

He went to a local range, set up the course of fire, and ran through it a few times. It should be no surprise that he shot well. So he started looking around for some type of practical shooting competition and found a club that shot IPSC. He watched a match and thought, *This looks like a lot of fun!*

In the early 1980s, Bruce was shooting well in local matches. He didn't travel much, mostly to upstate New York and New Jersey. By 1986, Bruce had joined the police force. While the pay was not grandiose, the vacation time was excellent. This allowed him to travel to shoot. Still, he stayed in the region; Vermont was as far as he generally went. Regardless, Bruce was successful enough to garner some attention from the industry. Austin Behlert, a pistolsmith who owned Behlert Precision, built some guns for Bruce. It was about 1986, when Caspian's Gary Smith saw him at a match and offered him some parts, if Bruce would

put the Caspian logo on his jersey. That was the beginning of a relationship that exists between the two today.

The late John Nowlin, an outstanding 1911 gunsmith from Oklahoma, took Bruce on as well. He invited Bruce to his shop and gave him a lesson on how to build guns and, most importantly, do trigger jobs on the 1911. Bruce told me, "By the time I left there, I was able to do great trigger jobs. The guns I took to Bianchi Cup were the sweetest one-pound triggers you ever felt. Having the best trigger was why my scores were so good." Since the early days, the rules were changed, and those ultra-light trig-

Clean shaven and ready for a clean run.

Bruce is not only an
amazing shooter, but an
outstanding gunsmith.

gers are no longer allowed.

Bruce is very open with his information about his career and the guns he shoots. If someone approaches him and asks about how he does so well, he will always tell them, even competitors. He preaches the basics, and those basics start with the trigger.

"So many instructors, especially when it comes to accuracy, make shooting harder than what it is. I'm a firm believer that 90 percent of shooting accurately comes down to squeezing the trigger correctly. If you can squeeze a trigger correctly, you're gonna have good shots."

Bruce also explained that a perfectly still gun is not required to hit the target.

"It's okay for it to wobble. Let it wiggle—just squeeze the trigger correctly. People look at you like, *What do you mean the gun's moving?* Yeah, it's *supposed* to move. Nobody can hold a gun perfectly still. Most people, when they first start, they try to, they see a perfect sight picture and they try to yank that trigger. They try to time the perfect shot. And it's never gonna happen. It's a losing strategy."

Bruce was quickly racking up the wins. He was also strategically choosing the matches that he shot.

"I was chasing the money," he admitted. "There was big money at the 1995 Masters Pistol."

The Masters International Pistol Championship was a winner-take-all annual match held at Pike Adams Sportsman Alliance Park, in Barry, Illinois.

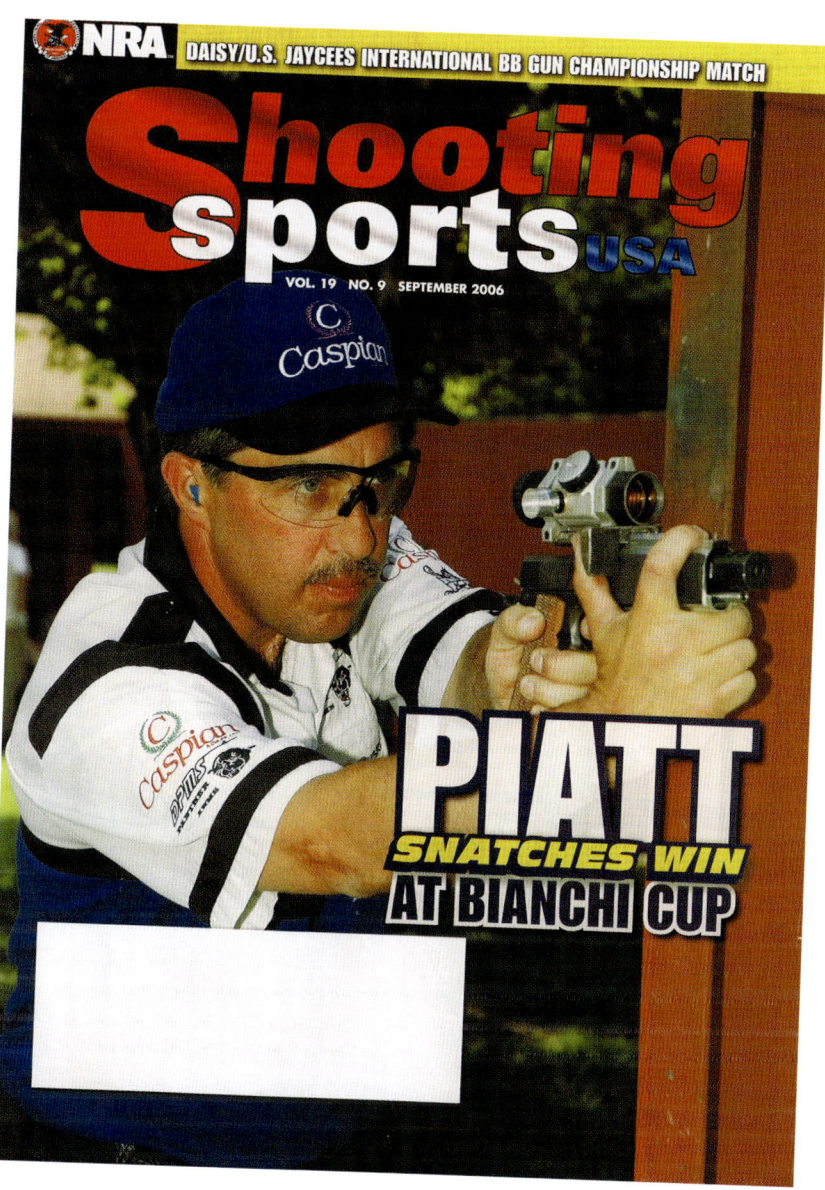

"That match was a lot of fun. We would shoot steel from all kinds of distances. There was also a stage where we would shoot out to 200 meters. That was great. There was also a bullseye-style stage."

While he is a skilled guy, he doesn't always win. In 1995, Jerry Barnhart won the Masters, while Bruce came in a close second.

"Jerry took home $100,000—I got nothing but a pat on the back."

Always in the hunt.

Since then, Doug Koenig has dominated the sport, with 17 wins to his name.

Like many shooters, Bruce grew up idolizing Jim Clark, arguably the greatest civilian bullseye shooter of all time. Bruce said to me, "When you consider the technology that they had then and the ammunition, what he accomplished was truly amazing.

"Jim Clark was always a gentleman. I remember I was down there at his range, practicing with his son, Jimmy Clark. He would always help—or sometimes just tease us. 'Just squeeze the trigger boys, just squeeze the trigger,' he would say with a laugh.

"He sure could shoot, though. Jerry [Miculek] said that one day he was at the range, practicing for the Masters, and Mr. Clark pulls up in a John Deere four-wheeler. When asked what he was doing, Jerry answered, 'Trying to shoot those darned four-inch targets.' Apparently, Mr. Clark, in his seventies at the time, hopped out and took the gun from Jerry, hand shaking like a leaf. *Bang, bang, bang, bang, bang*, and all five targets down. 'What's so hard, here?' he asked, and got back in to the four-wheeler and left laughing.

"I remember when I first met Lones Wigger for the first time, at the Sportsman's Team Challenge. I was stuttering. He was standing there owning a pile of Olympic gold medals and dozens of national championships. I was, literally,

John Bianchi with Bruce at a Bianchi Cup.

speechless."

No matter what discipline, Bruce uses a 1911.

"I have guns that are very heavy on purpose. My Open Bianchi gun has a shroud on it, and a Tungsten guide rod in order to make the front heavier, so it reduces some of the wobble. The gun is extremely heavy. On the other end of the scale is my 9mm for shooting steel; aluminum frame, Swiss cheese slide. It's meant for shooting 90-grain bullets at sub-1,000 feet. You can do anything with a 1911. Heck, I even have a titanium frame carry gun. You can do anything with it. And I have a .22 conversion. What can't you do with a 1911?"

For 3-Gun competition, Bruce shoots a .38 Super.

"I like the feeding aspect of the Super. I actually carry a 9mm barrel with me to matches, so that, if I ever have an ammunition problem, like it gets lost in shipping, I could always go to a store and buy some 9mm and just drop the barrel in the gun. And I use the same magazines out of the same gun and it'll work just fine.

"John Browning was a genius. He made that gun work for the cartridge length of the .45 ACP; it's no accident the .38 Super is the same length. The function of the .38 is simply better than a 9mm."

Bruce has some cool old bullseye guns, too.

"I have an old Giles bullseye gun. It has that unique 'wagon wheel' sight on it. That gun is in .38 Special, a very cool gun to have in your collection."

Caspian, being one of the most prominent manufacturers of 1911 parts, has been a big help to Bruce as a sponsor.

"I couldn't ask for a better sponsor. They are so supportive. Between Caspian and DPMS, I couldn't ask for better people behind me."

Apparently Gary Smith of Caspian has never told Bruce that he has to win. They told him to just mingle with his Caspian jersey on and "be Bruce.""

Of course, no one has to tell Bruce Piatt to win. He just does.

SCOTT McGREGOR: MAKING 3-GUN HISTORY

SCOTT McGREGOR IS A COMPETITOR in 3-Gun. Scott is also a big boy. This combination means that Scott shoots in Heavy Metal Optics, a division that requires its users to shoot the big guns. They can have one optic on the rifle, as opposed to Heavy Metal, which is iron sights only. Shotgun has to be a 12-gauge, semi-auto in Heavy Metal Optics versus a pump-action only in Heavy Metal. The capacity is limited to eight in the shotgun tube. Rifles must be .30-caliber or greater with a 20-round limit. Finally, the handgun has to be .44- caliber or greater and the magazine can't hold more than 10. Sound familiar? Yep, you got it. It was seemingly designed for the 1911.

The Heavy Metal Division of 3-Gun is also known as "He Man," and for good reason. The way I understand it, a fellow by the name of Eddie Rhodes wanted to get back to the combat heritage of firearms competition. His theory was that the race gun guys already had a place for their fast-shooting guns outfitted with compensators, optics, and lightened slides, but there really wasn't a place for the folks who like shooting full-power, heavy bullet cartridges.

The power factor for the He Man division was based on military ammunition, with the rifle segment based on .308 ball ammo. Same thing with the handgun, as it is based on .45 ACP power levels. The shotgun can only use slugs or buckshot. This is all to say that the He Man division was made for a large guy like Scott who clocks in at six feet three inches and 250 pounds on a good day.

Scott's hands are so large that he has to wrap around the trigger guard. It obviously works as evidences by the lack of muzzle flip.

One advantage of shooting the Heavy Metal of this somewhat new, but only recently super popular gun game, is that the equipment is cheap. Dad's old WWII .45 and the surplus M1 Garand are perfect for it. That's not to say it's a retro division. Scott started out with a Springfield TRP 1911 .45.

A cool thing about 3-Gun is the way that people help one another. Competitors often walk a stage ahead of time, discussing how they plan on approaching the different challenges. If you have not had the opportunity to walk a course

of fire with competitors, I suggest you do so. In my experience, the openness of information they share is unlike it is in any other shooting sport that I have seen. Heck, unlike any sport in general.

It was that attitude of cooperation that led Randy Luth, the founder of DPMS, to offer Scott a hand. He introduced him to some of the best in the business. This included the DPMS shooting team, which counted Bruce Piatt and Tony Holmes among its members.

Scott started watching what the people he was competing against were using, their holster, guns, everything. These super shooters were happy to help, especially when it came to their 1911s. Somewhere around 2006, Scott was talking to Bruce Piatt and Jim Clark, Jr. Jim Jr. has been an outstanding competitor in combat-oriented matches for years. He has also been a dominant 3-Gun competitor. Jim Jr. and Bruce were talking to him about building a high-capacity 9mm for USPSA and Steel Challenge use. While Clark Custom Guns is a legendary builder of 1911s, Bruce is also an outstanding 1911 gunsmith. Bruce built a gun for Scott, and it was a tack driver. He told me, "It's everything you would expect it to be from the five-time winner of the Bianchi Cup. It's tight and it's smooth, but, when Bruce built it, he didn't go for pretty. I think he used Brownell's Aluma-Hyde, but it's worn off in all the strategic places."

Scott says it looked great when he got it, but years of hard use has it looking a little rough these days. He said, "It still works great, but it isn't pretty anymore. Bruce says it looks 'salty,' and I guess he's right."

No longer a pristine example of the gunsmith's craft, Scott's prized high-capacity 9mm, built on a Caspian frame, does look a little shaggy. Thirty- or 40,000 rounds and countless competitions will do that.

That gun was the beginning of a lot of 1911s that Scott would shoot. Another great 1911, one that Scott is very proud of, is one built for him by a sponsor. Colt had partnered with a company called Bold Ideas, which was building the Colt competition rifle, an AR-15. Dennis Veilleux wanted Scott to shoot Colt pistols, too. While Colt has made a lot of .38 Supers, it had never made a high-capacity

9mm before. Veilleux had the Colt Custom Shop build one on a high-capacity frame.

This is something that simply is not done. For Colt to do what it did is such a divergence from standard practices, that no one believed Scott when he told them the story. He ended up getting an archive letter from the factory that lists the specific parts, including the frame, and named the gunsmith who built it. It also says, "Built for Scott McGregor for use in Three Gun Competition."

"To have an iconic company like Colt do that for me was one of the coolest moments in my shooting career. And the gun ranks right up there with the one built by a legendary shooter like Bruce. It is very humbling."

Scott loves all guns—Glocks, Smith & Wesson M&Ps, etc.—but, when it comes time to compete, he has a 1911 in his hand. For Tac-Ops, the tactical division of 3-Gun that allows optics, he has been shooting an STI Marauder. For Heavy Optics, the same as He Man, but allowing for scopes, red dots and the like, he uses one of the guns Colt built for him. And, when at the grocery, he might have a Kimber CDP in .45 ACP.

Scott comes by his love for the 1911 not only from competition and his belief that it is the best tool for the job. It also comes from his love of history. You see, Scott majored in history at Weber State University, in Ogden, Utah. The young lad, freshly transferred from a school in San Diego, was influenced by the town's most famous resident, John Moses Browning.

"My college apartment was just down from the canyon he used to use to go test fire his designs. Everything from the 1917 to the BAR to the 1911 was designed and tested right up the street from where I went to school."

Scott was a defensive lineman for the Weber State football team, the Wildcats.

"I had a great time playing football, and it helped me focus in school. It even got me engaged. But being in Ogden also stoked the passion of my love of firearms."

One must understand that John Moses Browning was born in Ogden, and, being there, you are unlikely to forget this fact. This is not to say that Browning is the only famous person from the town of less than 100,000 residents. Hal Ashby was born in Ogden, and he went on to direct many movies, including the Academy Award winning *In the Heat of the Night*. The Osmond family, its most prominent members being Donnie and Marie, were also from the little city. Former national security advisor to two presidents, Brent Scowcroft, was also from Ogden.

Still, visitors drive past 505 27th Street to look at the John Moses Browning's house where it still sits, looking much like it did when he lived there. The John M. Browning Firearms Museum is located at Union Station; it is a popular spot for tourists and historians alike. Heck, the 1911 is the official gun of Utah, the first state ever to make such a proclamation.

To a young, impressionable history buff like Scott, the heritage of the 1911 is not lost. Like most people who are into history, Scott has a favorite period.

"I love military history. I studied a lot of Russian history, starting with the Czarist times, right through the Revolution. Of course, the Soviet involvement in World War II was fascinating. This intersected with the American military

PHOTO COURTESY R. HARBIN

and the 1911.

"John Browning designed such a great machine [in the 1911]. It was reliable in the trenches of World War I, and, yet, 100 years later, it is still a great gun. That it is going strong in the shooting sports is a testament to the design.

"I have been blessed to have some great friends help me along the way. I remember Jerry Miculek pulling me aside and saying, 'It's a machine. Machines like lubrication. You don't run your car with a dry engine.'"

He also asked Jim Clark, Jr., how often to clean it. The answer he got was, "When it stops working."

With his love of history, being a 1911 guy might have seemed inevitable, but it wasn't. Scott looks at what equipment other people use, especially those skilled in whatever discipline he is trying to master.

"Not only do all the top competitors shoot a 1911, it just feels right."

Yep, it sure does.

CHAPTER 17

JULIE GOLOB: WONDER WOMAN WITH A GUN

F I WERE GIVEN THE TASK of creating the perfect ambassador for the shooting sports, I would create Julie Golob. Her accomplishments are second to none, her smile is sincere, and she is just downright nice. Does it hurt that she is a mom, a hunter, a foodie? Not at all. Former military? Another plus. Wrap it all in a lovely package, and I think that Smith & Wesson scored the ultimate hire, when it convinced her to be team captain of its shooting team. She is the all American girl.

Julie's father was a school teacher. He was the band director and music teacher in Seneca Falls, a tiny little hamlet in upstate New York. Hunting and fishing were family activities. Julie and her father spent many happy hours at the range. She was always working at the range, stapling targets, shagging brass, and working as a range officer. By age 14, she was inspired to start shooting competitively. Guess what handgun she used when she started her USPSA career?

It was so long ago, that she doesn't even remember what particular 1911 it was. She thinks back, "Probably a Colt, maybe a Springfield. I just don't remember." Whatever brand, it served this amazingly talented young woman well. In fact, she was shooting so well that, in 1995, she was recruited straight out of high school to the prestigious United States Army Marksmanship Unit (USAMU). This was the beginning of her career as a professional shooter, and she used her Army-issued 1911 to own the competition. In 1999, Julie won everything she entered, which was seven of the eight USPSA championships. She also knocked down the women's title at the World Speed Shooting Championship (commonly referred to as "Steel Challenge."), then back-to-back national titles in both USPSA Open and Limited divisions.

Could she have done all this without a 1911? Who knows, but probably not.

"I have always had short fingers, and a lot of guns just don't fit me," she told me. "The 1911 does." Add the fact that it is infinitely customizable, and it works for her. She continued, "Nineteen-elevens are like Harleys. That's the beauty of them. You can add all the bells and whistles—red dot optics, crazy safeties, magazine wells—all the things to make them fit you and work better for you."

Julie also says that the 1911 makes her a better competitor no matter what she is shooting.

"You have to be so perfect when you do a magazine change, even with a beveled mag well. You are fitting something that is so small and skinny into the gun. Your fundamentals have to be perfect. When you shoot any other gun, especially a double-stack with the magazines tapered at the top, it is so easy after a single-stack 1911." Or, put another way, "If you can reload a single-stack 1911, you can reload anything."

Julie loves the purity of plain-Jane 1911. USPSA hosts a single-stack event at PASA (Pike Adams Sportsman Alliance) Park. "It takes you back to the roots of shooting. You really have to be a great shooter to compete with a plain 1911. Sure, you can shoot a double-stack with a red dot, but take those things away. Just the pure frame with a small magazine well and iron sights. It defines your ability as a shooter."

While Julie may like the challenge of a bone-stock, iron sight 1911, it is not her normal gun. Just look at her new NRA Action Pistil Open fun guns. "They are tricked *out*!" she told me, in an excited tone.

The guns she's talking about are Pro Series 9mms from the Smith & Wesson custom shop. They are anything but stock, instead rocked out with an action pistol shroud. This is a device that allows the shooter to wrap their fingers around it, near the muzzle. This is particularly useful when shooting up against a bar-

When you are leading, it is easy to smile.

ricade. She is also accessorized with a stick shift mover base. This is a platform for an optic that adjusts via a lever, the stick shift. This allows the shooter to change the point of impact for long or short shots. Julie also favors a prone pad, which is much like a magazine well, except that it's flat across the bottom, designed to give the shooter a good base when shooting prone.

"The Smith & Wesson Performance Center always does a great job, but I really love these beasts! They are big and heavy and super accurate. They are a lot of fun to shoot!"

As prolific and successful as she is at the action pistol sports, Julie has also tried her hand at bullseye.

"One year, at Camp Perry, I shot .45-caliber service pistol, badly, I might add," she said with a laugh. Of course,

with her accomplishments, including more than 50 national, international, and world titles, her idea of "badly" probably isn't the same as mine.

"No beavertail, a trigger of at least four pounds, it's a real challenge," she said. Yes, the restrictions are onerous in bulleseye. Extended controls, such as slide stop, thumb safety or magazine release, are strictly forbidden. No ambidextrous safety is allowed. A commander style hammer is also a big no-no. Heck, you can't even have torx or Allen head screws holding your grips down.

"With the wind and the hundreds of other shooters watching, it is no easy feat." She said, "but I love the challenge."

Julie seems to love the challenges the shooting sports offer. And, best of all, she loves meeting and conquering them with one of her many trusty 1911s.

CHAPTER 18

JESSE TISCHAUER: THE NEW 1911 KID ON THE BLOCK

JESSE TISCHAUSER IS ON THE TOP RUNGS of the 3-Gun Nation tour, a USPSA competitor, son of an arms dealer, former Army staff sergeant. Yes, he is all of those things, but he is relatively new to the 1911.

Believe it or not, Jesse started shooting the 1911 only a few years ago, 2010, to be exact. His father had a World War II-era 1911, but neither of them never used it. His father was more of a revolver guy than anything else. Because of that, Jesse knew more about Colt Single Action Armys and Ruger Blackhawks than he did about John Moses Browning's masterpiece. Sure, when he was young he was part of the gun culture, but competition was the farthest thing from his mind.

"I considered myself a gun guy, but didn't have a ton of guns. Sure, I had my shotgun from when I was a kid. A rifle my dad left me. There were a couple of his pistols in the safe, too. There was really no reason for me to buy more guns. I had the ones I needed, and it wasn't like I was shooting a lot like I ha been when I was a kid back in Wisconsin. Up there, we hunted and shot all the time."

In 2009, Jesse's interest in competitive shooting began. He discovered USPSA.

"When I found competitive shooting, it really rejuvenated things. My interest in shooting began to grow to the point of becoming what you might call intense. That is one reason I encourage people to get into competitive shooting. It is not only a ton of fun and teaches great skills, it often gives you a use for the guns you already own."

Jesse Tischauser climbing the leader board

Like many, Jesse started with a Glock. It was cheap and reliable, as well as a tough gun. It served him well for a year or two, but, when he wanted to get serious in competitive shooting, it was time for a 1911.

"The first 1911 I ever owned was chambered in .40 S&W. I needed it to compete in a larger national level USPSA match in the Single Stack division. My gunsmith, Mike Cyrus, of Accurate Iron, built a gun for himself to beat up. It was a Frankengun. It was not pretty. In fact, it was ugly, but it ran like a champ." Jesse laughed, "It was a parts gun that he built out of stuff he had left over on his bench and from parts he picked up off of prize tables: STI fame, Caspian slide, and virtually no finish on the gun." He laughs at the memory. "I still have that gun. She's ugly, but she has always worked great when I needed her."

Frankengun opened the door and a stampede ensued.

"Next, I had Mike Cyrus build me a custom 1911-style gun. Since my interests had changed to 3-Gun, I went with a wide-body double-stack 2011 on an STI frame chambered in 9mm. This gun was *gorgeous*: Slide cuts, hard chrome finish and pretty much anything you can think of to make it fast. After shooting that one for a year, I had to have another, so,I had Mike build an even bigger and better version of the double-stack 9mm 3-Gun race pistol. I used the first one to practice with and the new one for matches."

Of course, then the floodgates opened.

"I started shooting other divisions in 3-Ggun and became classified in all six USPSA divisions. So, I needed more 1911s. I bought a couple of bone-stock STI Edges in .40 S&W and .45ACP, as well as a single-stack STI Spartan in .45 ACP. The .45s are for the two Heavy Metal divisions in 3-Gun and the .40 is for USPSA in Limited and Limited 10 divisions."

As with most things in the race gun game, nothing is left stock in its factory configuration. Jesse had Accurate Iron do trigger jobs and texture the grips on his guns to "slick 'em up." That kept him content for about another year. He then bought a five-inch SVI (Stayer Voight, Incorporated, markets its outstanding guns as the Infinity brand). After a week of shooting it, Jesse liked it so much that he ordered two more.

"The 1911 is such a great firearm. The 2011 is a really fun adaptation of that design. Then you have the wide body double stack Infinity pistols. They are works of art. They are truly custom pieces as you can have them any way you like. The only limitation is your imagination and your billfold.

Jesse's 1911 style gun acquisition binge was not over.

"Matt McLearn, a great guy who owns McLearn Custom Gun out in the Phoenix area, he built me open pistol with a red dot and compensator. It's basically set up for shooting Steel Challenge, but it's the same kind of gun for shooting 3-Gun Open division. I also had it built with a tactical frame, so that I could mount a Streamlight laser/light combo on it and run it in the new and really fun nighttime 3-Gun matches."

Once Jesse started shooting 1911s, that was it for his Glocks.

"I don't want to say anything bad about Glocks, M&Ps, XDs or any other plastic guns. There are still uses for them. But, if I am competing, I have a 1911 or a 2011 in my hands. If there are prizes and money on the line, I am going to be using that amazing single-action 1911 trigger.

"Here's the explanation I came up with as to why a 1911 is better than a polymer gun for competition—or any reason, for that matter. I look at it this way. If you align your sights perfectly every time while pulling the trigger perfectly every time, you will hit every target every time no matter the gun. But if you have a more accurate gun and a lighter shorter trigger, you will hit more targets when you don't align the sights perfectly and/or don't pull the trigger perfectly. A Glock won't make you miss more than a 2011 if you do your part. But a 2011 might help you miss less than with a Glock if you don't do your part."

Being a Johnny come lately to the 1911 scene, Jesse is no slave to tradition.

"I like the heft of a full-length dust cover, especially with a rail."

It seems part of his accessorizing he

attributes to some night matches put on by Crimson Trace.

"The 1911s I had didn't have a rail, so I couldn't put a light on it. I sold one, so as to get a rail gun."

Now he loves his S.V.I. with the tactical frame. He told me, "Even when not shooting night matches, I love shooting that gun. In 9mm, it is so soft recoiling and flat shooting. It is like competing with an airsoft or a pellet gun."

After shooting a few night matches, Jesse became a huge believer in the laser sights and weapon lights.

"I always thought that lasers were for people who didn't shoot often. Basically, good tools for less skilled shooters and those that don't practice. But boy was I wrong! You can hit your target while running much faster than you could ever do with iron sights or even a red dot. It doesn't matter what you are doing, running backwards or hanging around a corner or over an awkward barricade. It's also a great training tool. The trick to being a fast shooter is knowing how good of a sight picture is acceptable for any given target. It is really tough to keep a laser steady, especially under stress. With the help of a laser in dry-fire and in matches, I learned how much sight movement and misalignment is acceptable. It's the same thing with iron sights, but so much more obvious with the laser. The challenge in competitive action shooting is always to see how poor of a sight picture you can have and still get good hits on target. That is where the speed comes from."

So, while many of us love the 1911 at least partially for its history, some of the young guns love it simply because it works. New-fangled sighting systems, hanging lights off of them—it's all good. And with all that goodness, the 1911 has adapted itself to yet another generation.

CHAPTER

19

TED NUGENT: BEWARE THE HUNTER WITH A 10MM 1911

FOR ANYONE WHO HAS THE PRIVILEGE of knowing Ted Nugent, you know that there is no one like him, and he is unapologetically *Ted*. You might call him Uncle Ted, the Backstrap Assassin, the WhackMaster, or the Motor City Madman, but no matter what moniker you use, there is no doubt that what you see is what you get.

There has never been a man who has celebrated his life like Ted Nugent. I would bet that if Ted were to be reincarnated, he would beg to come back as Ted.

Ted loves guns, including the 1911.

"God knows, it's all been said about his Majesty John Browning, but I add a giant 'Ditto!' to all the exaltations and admiration the great man deserves. That his pistol is more popular today, more than 100 years after he designed it, is testimony to the ubiquitous capabilities and shootability and just functionality of his unbelievable timeless design. I gotta say it: God bless John M. Browning."

Of course, Ted can't stop there.

"You do have to hand it to the Bill Wilsons and the other 1911 specialists out there. There's no limit to where we can take the 1911 to upgrade and improve the original design. I think the scramble and flurry that exists in the mad scientist, ballistic shoot-'em-up world is something to adore, because all of us who love to shoot are beneficiaries of this kind of scrutiny and upgraded maniacal pursuit of perfection."

YAMIL SUED PHOTO

One of the 1911s that Wilson Combat customized for the WhackMaster.

While Ted is widely known for loving his Glocks, when he's hunting, he more often than not grabs one of his prized 1911s—and *always* in 10mm. It is his favorite handgun hunting round.

"The 10mm is a phenomenal round. It's proven by Evan Marshall's study to be the most effective one-shot stop self-defense round, and I am an adherent of genuflecting at the Jeff Cooper altar of the .45 ACP 1911. He developed the 10mm back after the 1986 Miami FBI shoot-out cluster*#$&—you know what I mean."

(In case you don't remember 1986, what Uncle Ted refers to is a shootout in Miami, where the agents outnumbered the bad guys four to one and yet two agents were killed and five were wounded. It was a very bad day, and a painful

lesson for anyone in law enforcement at the time.)

It has been said that Ted's evangelism concerning the 10mm Glock is what kept that model alive in Glock's lineup. But understand that Ted loves all guns. In fact, Ted isn't a gun snob at all.

"All guns are good. I don't think there has ever been a bad gun. It's just a matter of choice and picking, choosing, experimenting, and practicing. You have to fondle and beat up as many as you can so you find the ones that feel good. I think everybody has to find the right woman, the right gun, the right guitar, the right bow, the right truck, and the right dog."

The WhackMaster also had some words for those who take their enthusiasm too far.

YAMIL SHED PHOTO

"I wish that some of the 1911 aficionados would refrain from escalating into arguments that the 1911 is 'God' and nothing else is any good. It almost comes off as an anti-gun rant. We should celebrate all Second Amendment advocates, not just those with a preference for the 1911."

While few people shoot as often as Ted, who shoots daily, he preaches practice.

"Learn breathing and sight picture and squeeze and you can pull off some mind-blowing shots. Then you can start using some of the potential of the gun, especially a 1911 in 10mm." He goes on, "We just posted a video of a beautiful buck I killed with my Kimber 10mm. I was using some prototype Ted Nugent ammo, 165-grain stuff. It was a 90-yard

shot. Folks kind of got gaga about it, because the first time you pick up a pistol, you really can't hit the broad side of a barn from inside. It just takes practice, and lots of it.

"I love handgun hunting, and 10mm handguns are legitimate, ethical, capable big-game weapons."

This is something Ted has proven countless times, and no more so than when he took a Cape buffalo. He was at 30 yards and nailed him, cutting the vertebrae of the beast. Of course, as often as he hunts, that's just one tale he has about hunting with his beloved 10mm.

"I don't know how much more proof you need than a Cape buffalo, but I've killed many giant, fat, muscly zebras, kudu, American bison, and giant 600-pound wild hogs; the round is ter-

minal. I killed an elk at 125 yards running flat out. One shot. When that bullet hit the point of the shoulder of that running elk, it knocked him over like a .338 Win. Mag. Folks think I'm exaggerating, but I don't make this stuff up. Besides, it's on film. I probably shoot more big game with a 10mm than anybody who's ever lived, because I've been doing it since the round first became available. It is a legitimate big-game cartridge."

Ted has a lot of 1911s: Wilsons, Springfields, Paras, Colts, Remingtons, Smiths, CZs, STIs, Dan Wessons, Kimbers, and others.

"My STI Perfect Ten is a sniper. It is a genuine 100-yard pistol. The gun is just supremely accurate."

For a segment of his television show *Ted Nugent's Spirit of the Wild*, which airs on the Outdoor Channel, he killed two Sika stags from a ground blind at 50 and 60 yards.

"I was using my STI with some prototype Ted Nugent ammo, 150-grain stuff. You couldn't hit those animals any better using a .243 rifle with a scope. In the hands of a guy who trains and practices adequately, these are genuine, long-range big-game killers."

He doesn't even use extremely long barrels to hunt.

"The sight radius is longer, but it only has to be long enough. I have not experienced an advantage to the longer barrels. Obviously, you get a little more terminal velocity from the longer barrel, but I don't think flesh cares."

Ted tells the story of a hog hunt in Albany, Texas.

"We stalked this wide-open wheat field and were using a line of telephone poles to get us as close as we could to this little sounder of hogs. Later, we paced it off at 120 yards. I was going to try to get within bow range, but the lead sow's head went up, and we all froze. When her head went back down to feeding, I put the bow on the ground and I pulled out my then brand new Springfield 1911 long slide that Tim Reese at Springfield had designed just for me. Springfield never made a 10mm, but Tim had his guys put it together for me.

The first shot hit that sow right square in the shoulder, and she took off. As she started running, my second shot rolled her, running, at 130 yards. I turned that sniper of a pistol onto the others that were scrambling in every direction as fast as their little porker legs could carry them. There was a flurry of gunfire, and, when it was all said and done, I had killed six good hogs. Five were running, because after the first shot they were hauling ass. The furthest shot was paced at 200 yards. The last shot caught one that I hit in the belly running at about a 180 yards. We just stood there with our jaws dropped. If it wasn't on film with witnesses, I'd be called the biggest liar in the world."

Ted had one more thing to say about it.

"I don't think you need any more proof of the functionality, the ergonomics, the terminal firepower of the 10mm and the design of the 1911. These guns are snipers."

And if a gonzo guitar player who wrote *Wango Tango* can do it, so can you.

RAZOR DOBBS: HANDGUN HUNTING SENSATION

I HAVE GOT TO TELL YOU, I have a ton of respect for people who lead their lives on their own terms. Razor Dobbs, an Outdoor Channel hunting sensation, is one of those people. If you ask him, he will give a lot of credit to his friend and mentor, Ted Nugent. Of course, it takes more than a teacher; it takes a student who wants to learn.

Razor met Ted when he was going to Texas Tech, and they became fast friends. It wasn't long before they were travelling to Africa together, to Zimbabwe, where they hunted exotic beasts. It was soon after that adventure the WhackMaster asked, "Why don't you come work for me?"

"I moved to Michigan, where Nugent lived at the time, and moved in with the family," Dobbs told me. "Officially, I was his assistant. We went on music tours, I worked in the office, I worked on the magazine, and I hunted like a crazy maniac—and I soaked it all in."

Razor describes it like going into the military.

"It was intense, and I learned so much. I was already a hunter and shooter, but I went to the next level. Looking back, the thing I most cherish about the experience is that I really learned to work."

Razor says he will always be grateful for the lessons. Being in the world of that crazy guitar player who wrote *Cat Scratch Fever* was inspirational. He wanted to travel the world and hunt, sharing his experiences with others. As you would expect, The Motor City Madman was supportive.

One of many whitetails Razor has taken with his trusty Dan Wesson 10mm.

"'Razor, if you want to do it, don't let anything stand in your way,' he said to me."

Razor didn't.

"There wasn't even an Outdoor Channel back then. I quit working for Ted and focused on what I am doing now, making videos for the Internet and writing."

Razor was and is a big bow hunter, but he also learned to love handgun hunting. Like many bow hunters, he straps a handgun on his hip. Some carry a handgun simply for protection, others in case they need to finish off a wounded animal. A few will employ the handgun if

they can't get close enough to get a shot with the bow. Razor is of the mind that all three are legitimate reasons to carry a handgun.

He started with a Smith & Wesson chambered in .357 Magnum, but anyone who spends time around the Backstrap Assassin soon becomes enthralled with the 10mm.

After a while, the handgun became less of a backup weapon for Dobbs and more of a primary means of taking game. He still loves bow hunting, but the challenge of handgun hunting truly excites him. It wasn't long before the Smith

One of countless hogs that have been taken with Razor's Dan Wesson 1911.

Razor and his nilgai.

& Wesson was replaced with a Glock 10mm, and then, after many animals had been taken with that second gun, he finally got a 1911. It was a Dan Wesson Razorback, an *outstanding* 10mm.

Razor was intimidated by it at first.

"It just worked completely different from the Glock 10mm I was used to. I remember being at my house. I made sure it was clear and that there was no ammunition in the area, and I just sat down and messed with it. Basically, I studied and manipulated it, working the thumb safety, practicing trigger pulls, and doing magazine changes. I played with it until we became friends."

He then started reading and studying about the gun.

"In order to learn to fly that baby, I had to swallow my ego and start from the ground up." Among the things he learned was the amazing quality of the Dan Wesson.

"The Razorback is a Ferrari, compared to everything I had shot before. The fit and finish is second to none, and the ac-

The 10mm takes an elk.

Razor and his huge ram.

curacy is amazing!"

Dobbs lives on a ranch and carries this Dan Wesson daily. He doesn't baby it.

"It wasn't that long ago that I didn't even *want* a 1911. I heard that they are finicky, and I don't have time for that. With just a little maintenance, this Razorback never misses a beat. Of course, you have to use the right rocket fuel.

"There is virtually nothing you can buy over the counter that is full-power [in 10mm] these days. It used to be that only CorBon made full-power 10mm, but even it downloaded them."

When asked why he didn't roll his own, Razor answered, "I am not a reloader. I am an unloader.

"I had been asking around where I could find full-power 10mm. A buddy walked into my office and dropped a box of Double Tap 10mm on my desk. When I asked what it was, he explained it to me.

"Apparently, I was not the only one frustrated. DoubleTap was started because it couldn't get full power 10mm. Now it has a full line, and it is great ammo. I became such a Double Tap evangelist, that the company started sponsoring me."

By this time, Dan Wesson had discontinued the gun, but enthusiasm like Razor's is infectious. Razor has used that pistol exclusively as his sidearm. Not only does he carry it every day, he has also used it on television, talked about it on social media, and featured it in his videos. Dan Wesson now offers the 10mm 1911 solely because of Razor and his outspoken love for the gun.

Razor is always asking questions and trying to learn. When the bullet doesn't pass through the animal, he always tries to recover and weigh it. He told me, "I think I've found the ultimate loads for that 10mm, a DoubleTap that's loaded with a Barnes 155-grain bullet. It's just incredible. When you dig it out, it looks like a marketing photograph of how their bullets are supposed to perform." The bullets look like mushrooms, but with leaves splaying out in picture perfect fashion.

Test it on live game? Yes he has. A lot of it. He shot 13 whitetails in 2013, as well as two or three Axis bucks. In addition, he also took a nilgai and countless hogs.

"We were hunting whitetail and this nilgai buck came cruising by," he said. For those unfamiliar with nilgai, they are huge beasts, the largest of the Asian antelopes. The bucks can weigh in at more than 600 pounds. This is a very large animal. In fact, I am told that many ranches will not allow anything smaller than .300 Win. Mag. to be used. The reason is that the animals have a thick dermal shield over the shoulder and neck. Also, the organs are farther forward than in a whitetail. Shooting close to the shoulder joint is required.

"I had to shoot him right in the sweet pocket, right above the bottom of the leg bone and right below the shoulder blade, straight into the heart. He didn't go 50 yards before he collapsed."

These days, Razor has achieved his dream and stars on his own television show, *Razor Dobbs Alive*. The Outdoor Channel describes him travelling the

DAN WESSON 1911s

There have been many incarnations of Dan Wesson over the years, some good, some bad, and a lot in between. That all changed, in 2005, when CZ USA purchased the beleaguered company. Since that time, the quality of its 1911s has been nothing short of exemplary.

Like all Dan Wesson guns, the 10mm, which the company calls the Razorback, has no MIM (metal injection molded) parts and is hand-fit to amazing tolerances. Quite frankly, the Dan Wesson that sits on my desk as I write this is as tight and lovely as any of the full custom guns I have tested for this book—and yet is priced the same as some famous name 1911s that are assembly line produced guns filled with MIM parts.

Bang for the buck, Dan Wesson rocks.

The Dan Wesson Razorback is very accurate.

Score:
Sika 0/10mm 1

globe and hunting while meeting up, "with a coterie of crazy characters." This is not only accurate, you have to give them credit for the use of the word "coterie." On his show, one of his most popular handgun shots was taking a huge elk at 55 yards. He drilled it three times, and it collapsed.

"I had so much confidence in the Dan Wesson 1911 that there was no doubt in my mind he was going down. I got a good sight picture and nailed him right in the heart. He spun and I hit him again. Before I knew it, I'm running up to him, doing a tactical reload, simply from force of habit. He had already fallen dead into the pond."

Handgun hunting with the 1911 is not a novelty for Razor. He estimates he has killed about 40 big-game animals with his 1911.

"Once I learned that the gun was perfect, that I am flawed, it all became easy. No excuses, I own it. If it isn't working right, I need to learn and improve or just practice more." Razor went on, "The gun's limits are way beyond the shooter's, so it's best not to think that there *are* limits."

Razor Dobbs and the author agree that Dan Wesson is the best custom 1911 value.

PART IV

THE MODERN 1911

THE CALIBERS

F YOU ARE READING THIS BOOK, you probably think the 1911 is a great platform for launching bullets. Like most gun folks, you probably have more than one caliber you like, and it just so happens that your favorite gun is ideal for launching a lot more than just the .45 ACP. Sure, the original, and many would argue the best, is the good old .45, in fact old timers are likely to call 1911s "forty fives." But there is a plethora of cartridges that can be hurled downrange by a 1911.

.17 MACH II

The .17 Mach II was created by Hornady and CCI. It is not to be confused with the .17 Hornady Magnum Rimfire, also known as the .17 HMR. No, the Mach II is the venerable .22 Long Rifle necked down to .17-caliber. Created as a more reasonably priced alternative to the .17 HMR, it quickly found a home among varminters, small-game hunters and benchrest shooters.

Of course, the .17 Mach II is likely to be found in guns produced by Volquartsen, Anschütz, or Savage. Still,

Kimber was convinced to build a 1911 in this round. It was really kind of silly. After all, the 1911 really isn't the kind of gun to maximize the advantages of the round.

While perhaps not a great round for the 1911, the .17 Mach II is a very cool round nonetheless. Out of a rifle, it is very flat shooting. In addition, it is a very accurate cartridge. I am told that it is easily capable of 1-MOA (minute of angle) out of a good barrel. Not bad. Not bad at all.

.22 LONG RIFLE

Of course, the plinker, the .22 LR, is widely available. Not only are there .22 LR conversion kits, there are also dedicated .22 1911s. Of those dedicated .22s, many will argue that they are not truly 1911s, as they are not of the same design, while others will say that, since they fit in the same holsters, they are close enough.

The conversion kit has been around for a long time. Actually, the earliest version dates back to before World War II. Then and today, the conversion kits have had reliability issues, but a skilled gunsmith can get them running pretty well. Pushing back the weight of the slide is an issue for the tiny little cartridge; a mega-light recoil spring is required.

There are literally dozens of kits available. Some are of questionable quality, others are amazingly good. Personally, I do not see a good reason for a kit. The main reason is that no matter what attributes the kit has, it is still trying to push back full-strength hammer springs, and they're often pain to convert. Besides, the good kits are often more expensive than a dedicated .22. Get the gun for the job.

.224 BOZ

Back the 1990s, someone got the idea of necking down a 10mm to .223 with the thought of making a round with a lot of velocity and, thus, the ability to defeat body armor. I am told that it worked and worked well. I am also told that there were 1911 conversion kits in this short-lived, now defunct caliber. Like the unicorn and an honest politician, I have never seen one.

.30 LUGER

While not common in the United States, the .30 Lugar is fairly popular in other countries. I have read that this is because many countries ban the use of military calibers for use by their general publics; such civilians have to adapt. I am not completely sure that this is the reason, as I can't keep up with all of our own laws, let alone those of other countries. The bottom line is that if you're traveling, you might come across one of these conversions.

9MM LUGER

The 9mm 1911 is, perhaps, the most popular cartridge that the 1911 is chambered for. The reason for this is because of the gun games. Whether you are shooting IDPA, USPSA, Steel Challenge, 3-Gun, or many of the other gun games, the 9mm makes a lot of sense. With low recoil, easy access to ammunition, and cartridge efficiency, a 9mm 1911 is a very cool gun.

Of course, the 9mm is the most popular cartridge sold in the United States, period, and the 1911 is a mega-popular handgun, so it is not just the gamers who love the combination. I had the pleasure of carrying a great Wilson Combat CQB Compact in 9mm. The gun was easy to carry, hyper accurate, reliable as gravity, and pointed better than a full-size 1911. I would happily have that gun on my hip right now.

While the 9mm does not have the power of a .45 ACP, it is a very good round and the lack of recoil, even with +P and +P+ ammunition, is quite manageable in the small package. Another advantage is that the short barrel makes it easy to maintain sight discipline. Bill Wilson loves compacts, because both the front and rear sight are more easily kept in alignment, especially with aging eyes.

This is not to say that all 9mm 1911s are compacts. I shoot IDPA matches with a fellow who does a very credible job with a full-size, five-inch, 1911. While it is his range toy, I would not bet against him using that firearm when the flag goes up.

.38 SPECIAL

Many of the early bullseye guns were .38 wadcutters. While not prized for their reliability, they were very accurate, and the wadcutter bullets made scoring easy, because of the nice crisp holes they punched in paper. While not the inventor, Jim Clark, arguably the finest civilian bullseye shooter in history, was known for his .38 wadcutter bullseye guns. Of course, he was not the only one to do the conversions. Many of the classic, pioneers of the 1911 were producers of bullseye guns, and .38 wadcutter was oft the choice.

9X23MM WINCHESTER

Want .357 Magnum performance out of your 1911? Well, Winchester has a cartridge just for you. I am told that it developed the cartridge for USPSA and IPSC, so that the cartridge had the ability to make Major power factor in a 9mm cartridge. Basically, Winchester was aiming to produce a .38 Super replacement. Power factor, of course, is a way to separate shooters and even the playing field. You can figure out power factor by multiplying the bullet weight in grains by its muzzle velocity in feet per second, then

dividing by 1,000. Of course, you can't shoot anything smaller than .40-caliber in any division and make Major in any division except Open.

Major requires a power factor of 165 or higher. A 125-grain bullet traveling at 1,400 fps has a power factor of 175. That makes major.

Personally, I have never seen a competitor using a 9x23mm Winchester, but hey, it was one of Winchester's goals. Another factor was "coolness." Let's face it, a mega-hot 9mm is just neat. Besides, it was a direct competitor of the .357 SIG.

There is nothing magic about the cartridge. It is quite simply a 9mm Luger with a longer case. The brass is 22.86 millimeters in length instead of 19.15. Sure, Winchester stiffens it up, but the case head diameters, shoulders, taper, extractor rims are exactly the same.

This baby cooks. Fast and flat shooting, it is a very accurate round. It's a very nice target gun, but do not overlook its defensive capability. While it never caught on like .357 SIG did, this would be an ideal law enforcement or defense round.

.357 MAGNUM

Want .357 Magnum performance out of your 1911 and don't want some "pretender" like the 9x23 mm Winchester? Dan Coonan makes one. Yep, you are reading that right. Dan Coonan got a wild hair in college and decided to build a .357 1911. Why? Why not? He liked the .357 and he liked the 1911. Why not combine the two? The engineering was pretty straightforward. The biggest issue was creating a dependable magazine.

He went with a link-less barrel, which will have many 1911 purists shudder and

A Coonan .357 Magnum is a handful to shoot.

whisper words like "heathen," but the design is similar to that of the Browning Hi-Power. It allows the barrel to tilt downward, which is a superior design. Yes, I said it.

The gun feels a little strange in your hand, but the .357 is tamed nicely in the heavy gun. It is a lot of fun.

.357 SIG

What do you get when you cross a .40 Smith & Wesson and a 9mm Parabellum? The .357 SIG. Yes, SIG Sauer decided to neck down the .40 to accept the .355-inch projectile. It is said that its goal

was to replicate the .357 Magnum performance. If that was in fact the goal, it was achieved. The 125-grain bullet boogies downrange at 1,450 feet per second. This is virtually identical to .357 Magnum performance. It is also a positive thing that the recoil is relatively mild, especially out of a 1911. To my hand, it feels about like the .40 Smith & Wesson from whence it was born.

The ammunition is pricy and the necked case makes it hard to reload. Because of this, .357 SIG has not seen a lot of popularity among civilians. Law enforcement, on the other hand, since they do not have to worry about spending, are very high on the round. It is flat shooting and has enough velocity for hollowpoints to expand reliably after good penetration.

.38 SUPER

See the longer and interesting story of this round at the end of this chapter.

7.62X25MM TOKAREV

Why would someone want to convert a 1911 to 7.62x25mm? My guess is because there are millions of rounds of surplus ammunition in that caliber. Maybe not in the United States, but in Soviet Bloc countries. The round itself is nothing special, but it was widely produced, so, having a 1911 that shoots it makes a certain amount of sense.

10MM

What do you get when a bunch of FBI agents get shot because they were outgunned? That's right, FBI agents in Miami got into a shootout with some bank robbers. Most of the agents had 9mm Smith & Wessons, probably Model 459s. It's a long and fascinating tale, if not also tragic, but the bottom line is that even though the Feds outnumbered the bank robbers four to one, two of the agents were killed and five were wounded. There was a lot of blame to go around; some of what happened was just bad luck. Either way, it was obvious the 9mm wasn't cutting it.

At this time, the legend himself, Jeff Cooper entered the scene, stage left, with a Bren 10. Well, actually, there is more to the story than that.

Cooper had been enlisted to develop the 10mm years before, in 1980. The result was a fairly hot 10mm cartridge in a CZ design built by Dornaus and Dixon.

The 10mm quickly became the round of the hour. Colt introduced the Delta Elite in 10mm. Smith & Wesson got the FBI contract with its 10mm Model 1076. The Bren 10 didn't make it long; an attempt to resurrect the gun failed.

.40 SMITH & WESSON

What do you get with when you cross a bunch of FBI agents who can't handle recoil of a 10 mm? That's right, the .40 S&W. After the 1986 Miami shootout debacle, the Feds went looking for a new cartridge and soon adopted the 10mm. The only problem was that when the paper pushers were asked to control the 10mm, they failed miserably. So, after wasting millions of taxpayer dollars outfitting agents with guns they couldn't hit the broad side of a barn with, they needed a new plan. What did they do? First, they lightened the load in the 10mm and called it the "FBI Lite." It wasn't long before Winchester and Smith & Wesson decided that as long as they were putting a smaller powder charge in the case, they could shorten it, thus the .40 Smith & Wesson was born.

The shorter overall cartridge length made the round quite easy to adapt to existing 9mm gun platforms, so most gun manufacturers almost immediately embraced the new cartridge. It wasn't long before the .40 became a most popular law enforcement round. It isn't just cops who like their .40s these days. The .40 S&W is also the smallest round that will make Major power factor in USPSA.

The general civilian market has not embraced the .40 S&W as strongly as the competitive community, but retired police handguns seems to be changing that trend. You see many departments change their handguns on a regular basis. Even though the guns might not have been shot much, they have been carried a lot and show a lot of wear. These guns can be pretty amazing bargains.

Will the .40 S&W ever catch the 9mm in popularity? Probably not, but it's heading that direction.

.400 CORBON

Like a lot of newly introduced cartridges, the .400 CorBon is the answer to a question that not many were asking. It is a .45 ACP case necked down to 10mm (.400). The increased velocity and low pressure seemed to be a nice combination, and the resulting round performed well. While the case size limits the projectile to 165 grains, still, cooking along at 1,450 fps is nothing to sneeze at. Reports are that it is an accurate round and has less recoil than the 10mm, whose ballistic performance was the benchmark for the round's designer Peter Pi.

Even though the conversion from .45 ACP to .400 CorBon was a drop in operation, not many did so. Is the .400 CorBon going the way of the .40 AE and the .41 Magnum? Yeah, probably.

.41 ACTION EXPRESS

The .41 AE had a short life as a cartridge, and it is now all but gone. While I am unaware of any companies that produced any dedicated .41AE guns in the 1911 platform, there were some conversion kits out there.

The round was supposed to replicate the .41 Magnum and truly did pretty well

at that. In fact, it was a good round, but failed to get any traction. What few guns that were produced for it, including the 1911 conversion kits, were soon phased out.

Is that fair? Nope. But remember, Tesla was on the right side of the direct current versus alternating current debate—but Edison won.

.45 GAP

Gaston Glock wanted a round that would be easier to engineer compact guns around, so he dialed up his buddies at CCI/Speer to develop the round. They came up with the .45 GAP (Glock Automatic Pistol). The only true advantage of this cartridge is that the depth from the front to the rear of the grip can be cut down. This makes the gun a little easier to get small hands around. It's not really a huge advantage, as the .45 ACP is already pretty short, but hey, who am I to question Gaston? He changed the way we think about guns. Sadly, for him, his cartridge has not had wide appeal. Oh well, guess that "Glock Perfection" thing isn't universal.

.460 ROWLAND

A fellow named Johnny Ray Rowland wanted a big boom. He got it with this round. With the idea that he could get .44 Magnum power out of a .45 ACP, he did just that. He had the venerable Starlight Brass produce the cases. They are just a little longer than a standard .45 ACP, a sixteenth of an inch. This is the same reasoning as to why the .357 Magnum case is longer than the .38 Special. The extra case length prevents the more powerful round from being chambered in a .45 ACP gun. Interestedly enough, the overall cartridge lengths of the two cartridges are the same. The bullet is just set deeper in the .460 Rowland.

Since the cartridge is the same length, standard 1911 magazines can be used—but, trust me, the rest of the gun needs some beefing up. Johnny Ray turned to Clark Custom Guns to help with the conversion kit. It is impossible to stack enough spring to take the robust cartridge, so a compensator is required.

This cartridge is a beast. Pushing a 230-grain bullet at 1,340 fps is no small feat. The 40,000 psi (pounds per square inch) is almost double that of a standard .45 ACP. If you ever had the desire to take down large game with a handgun, this just might be your round.

.50 GI (GUNCRAFTER INDUSTRIES)

"Why do you carry a .45?"

"Because they don't make a .46"

True, but they make a .50. This giant pumpkin of a round was invented by a couple guys who must have said, "The .45 ACP is a great round, but it doesn't punch a big enough hole." That's right, the guys at Guncrafters, Alex Zimmerman and Vic Tibbets, decided to make a new cartridge that would launch a boulder from a purpose-built 1911. With projectiles ranging from 185-grains to a whopping 300, this thing is a monster. While a low-pressure round, not unlike the .45 ACP that inspired it, its superb mass hits hard. Even though it is mega slow—some loads move as lethargically as not much more than 700 fps—it pounds the target like a sledgehammer. It was designed as a self-defense round, and there is no reason why it would not

fill the roll perfectly. Guncrafters sells brass, dies and, in addition to 1911s, Glock conversions.

Of course, there are a lot of one-of wildcat rounds I've missed. After all, the 1911 is wildly popular, so, it's no surprise that virtually every conceivable cartridge can be launched from John Browning's baby.

You might have noticed that I omitted the most obvious 1911 cartridge, the .45 ACP. Why? The round is so ubiquitous that one might even suggest it requires no mention. Heck, many call any 1911 a "forty-five," much as so many colas are referred to as a "Coke" and any tissue is called "Kleenex." Still, let's talk abou thtis round for a minute.

John Taliaferro Thompson served in the Spanish American War as an ordnance officer. He was not a man to be trifled with. Whether he was forming an unofficial Gatling Gun unit, moving tons of supplies, or overseeing the development of the Springfield Model 1903, he got the job done well and efficiently. In a time when logistical problems plagued the military, his star shined brightly and rose fast.

It was not long before Thompson became chief of the Small Arms Division of the Ordnance Department, as it was looking to replace the .38 Special. General Thompson wanted a "man stopper." This culminated into the famous Thompson Legarde Tests of 1904, held to determine what should be the cartridge for the military.

A new cartridge was deemed needed after the .38 Long Colt hadn't cut in in the Philippine Insurrection of 1902. The Moro revolutionaries were very tough; often times, even with several .38 Long Colt rounds in them, they just kept com-

Defense ammunition from Wilson Combat.

ing. As General "Blackjack" Pershing said, the Moro warrior was, "absolutely fearless, and once committed to combat, he counts death as a mere incident." Legarde recounted in his book, Gunshot Injuries: How They are Inflicted, Their Complications and Treatment, the story of a man that shot repeatedly with the .38 Long Colt.

Was shot four times at close range in a hand-to-hand encounter by a .38-caliber Colt's revolver loaded with U.S. Army regulation ammunition. He was finally stunned by a blow on the forehead from the butt-end of a Springfield carbine.

In 1904, Col. Thompson and Maj. Legarde staged a set of tests around several rounds, which included the .476 Eley, 7.65x22mm Parabellum, 9x19 Parabellum, .38 Long Colt, .45 Colt (now know as the .45 Long Colt), and the .455 Webley. The party was held at the Union Stock Yards, in Chicago.

And what a party it was. On the first day they shot cows, seven to be exact, through the lungs and through the intestines. If the cow didn't die quickly enough, they would kill it with a sledgehammer. PETA would go nuts today.

On day two, they not only shot another 16 or so cattle, but a couple horses, too.

They also hung human cadavers from a rope and measured the "swing" of the body when bullet struck. Macabre aside, they determined that, as Col. Legarde reported, "resistance and destruction of tissue, which are so intimately associated with shock effects—were invariably greater when a larger caliber bullet was used. ..." It seems that the larger rounds would drop the animals to their knees in three to five shots. The smaller rounds would take as many as 10 and still sometime fail to drop the beasts of burden.

While it should be obvious that current "scientific standards" were not met, even then they were criticized for being sloppy. Whether or not that criticism was deserved, the test organizers still determined that smaller diameter projectiles did not perform as well as larger ones.

The Board was of the opinion that a bullet, which will have the shock effect and stopping effect at short ranges necessary for a military pistol or revolver, should have a caliber not less than .45. ... None of the full-jacketed or metal-patch bullets (all of which were less than cal. .45) showed the necessary shock effect or stopping power for a service weapon. ... We are not acquainted with any bullet fired from a hand weapon that will stop a determined enemy when the projectile traverses soft parts alone. The requirements of such a bullet would need to have a sectional area like that of a 3-inch solid shot, but the recoil from which when used in hand weapons would be prohibitive. ... Finally the Board reached the conclusion that the only safeguard at close encounters is a well-directed rapid fire from nothing less than a .45-caliber weapon. With this end in view soldiers should be drilled to fire at moving targets until they have attained proficiency as marksmen.

In addition, Thompson and Legarde concluded that the round not only be .45-caliber or greater, but that it be at least 230 grains. Other recommendations included were that the magazine hold no less than six rounds and the trigger be no less than six pounds.

Since the recommendation was made that no new service pistol should be considered in less than .45-caliber, Colt would have to adapt. John Browning had been working with Colt on a .41-caliber round. Turns out it wasn't a big deal to increase the size to .45. In a brilliant move, Colt created the exact same case head dimensions of the .30-06. Good information to know, if you ever want to cut down cases for your 1911.

The .45 ACP was an effective round, low pressured, yet the 230-grain round-nose bullet makes a nice wound channel—or a horrible one, depending on your perspective. Ballistically, it is not an accurate cartridge. Ed Brown said that he tested dozens of barrels, and the guns are more accurate than the round. In fact, he only guarantees his guns are more accurate than the ammunition. That said, some brilliant ballisticians, such as Philip Massaro, can and do coax some serious accuracy out of the "low and slow" round.

One thing that is undeniable is the .45 ACP's reputation for stopping power, even if it is overstated. A friend of mine said he carries a .45 ACP 1911 because "even a shot to the arm will knock them down." While I tried to explain the fallacies of his opinion, I saw in his eyes that my words had no effect. The .45 is magic to him.

He is not alone. We all hear things like "The .45 ACP is like 9mm, but made for adults." Or "I carry a .45, because shooting twice is just silly," and the silly "A 9mm may or may not expand, but a .45 will never shrink!" My personal favorite: "It's a man's round in God's gun!"

Of course, the legend was grown out of true stories, so it's all rooted in fact. Just how effective the .45 ACP is can be gleaned from looking at Medal of Honor recipient, Thomas Baker, who was in the Battle of Saipan. His heroics are well documented, as are his use of his 1911. Of course, we cannot just blow by some of Sargent Baker's heroics to tell only of the .45 and his 1911; you have to understand that Thomas used a bazooka—a bazooka!—and risked his life to take up a position close to the enemy, which was laying down heavy fire. He knocked them back and saved his company. On a later day he, single handedly killed 12 Japanese soldiers, then came across another six, which he also dispatched.

On July 7, 1944, Baker was guarding a perimeter, when several thousand enemy soldiers attacked, 3,00 to 5,000 is the estimate given. He was seriously wounded, but refused to leave. In fact, he refused to let a fellow soldier carry him in retreat. He demanded that he be left, sitting back against a tree to support him. Later, his body was found with an empty 1911; slide locked back. Around him were eight dead Japanese soldiers, victims of the eight .45 ACP rounds that had been in his 1911.

No one would argue that story is an amazing example of a great man's heroism. In it, the effectiveness of the cartridge is not lost. Such stories have elevated the legend of the .45 to mythological status—and that status is unlikely to change.

THE "NEW" HISTORY OF THE .38 SUPER AUTOMATIC +P CARTRIDGE

A SPECIAL SECTION BY BRAD MILLER

The semi-rimmed .38 Super Automatic   Automatic.1 The "old" .38 Automatic was

Colt "Super .38" Automatic Pistol
CALIBER .38

General Specifications:

CALIBER: .38 for the .38 Rimless, Smokeless Cartridge.

LENGTH OF BARREL: 5 inches.

LENGTH OVER ALL: 8½ inches.

STOCKS: Checked Walnut.

TRIGGER: Checked.

ARCHED HOUSING: Checked.

FINISH: Full Blued.

WEIGHT: 39 ounces.

CAPACITY OF MAGAZINE: 9 Cartridges.

Modeled after that most famous of all Automatic Pistols — the Colt Government Model .45 — this new Super .38 bids fair to match its famous brother in all that a well made powerful Arm can do. It has every merit a gun could possibly possess — backed by over 93 years' experience of the oldest and most famous manufacturer of firearms in the world — makers of Colts since 1836. A grip that is certain, an action that is positive and Safety Locks that simply cannot fail — every outstanding feature of the already proven Colt .45 Automatic is embodied in this new Super .38, and to them has been added the distinct advantage of the .38 caliber automatic cartridge with its exceptionally high velocity of about 1200 foot seconds.

Special Features

The new Colt Super .38 Automatic Pistol will be hailed with unstinted appreciation by the Hunter of Big Game, the Trapper, the Explorer and Target Shooter. Thoroughly tested in the hands of those who recognize a perfect fire arm, the new Colt Super .38 Automatic Pistol has shown an enviable record of results.

With the one exception of caliber, the Colt Super .38 is identical in construction with the Colt .45 Government Model. It is equipped with both manual and automatic Grip Safety Locks exactly the same as the .45 — the Arched Housing, extension horn on grip and quick magazine release.

Fig. 2: Colt's 1929 Catalog

Cartridge." The cartridge drawings are labeled ".38 Automatic Colt Cartridge."

The 1929 Colt's catalog specifically indicates the caliber for the Super .38 Automatic Pistol as ".38 Rimless, Smokeless." This is the exact same name used to describe the cartridge for the Model 1900 series pistols (*Sheldon, 1987*). Again, new gun, old cartridge.

(Fig. 3) The velocity of the .38 Automatic cartridge with a 130-grain bullet in the 1928 Colt's advertisement was 1,190 fps. This was typical for this cartridge at the time, according to Douglas Sheldon (*1997*). He writes, "Contrary to popular belief, the cartridge ballistics were not changed in 1929 for the new model [Colt Super .38 pistol] ... ." Evidence from that time supports this claim. First, there is no mention in the ads of a new cartridge called the .38 Super Automatic. Second, ballistics for the cartridge in the ad match ballistics of the .38 Automatic at the time.

(Fig. 4) Sheldon (*1997*) notes that, "The initial specifications in the year 1900 called for a velocity of 1,260 fps with the Model 1900's six-inch barrel. Up until the introduction of the Super .38 Model, the velocity listed by cartridge manufacturers varied from time to time between approximately 1,160 and 1,280 fps."

A review of the Colt .38 Automatic pistol, Model of 1900, that was published in *Shooting and Fishing* magazine April 19, 1900 (*reported in Haven and Belden, 1940*) also says that the cartridge velocity was 1,260 fps, with some velocities being run up to 1,350 fps.

Neither Sheldon (*1997*), in his reference to the 1900 specifications of the .38 Automatic, nor the Shooting and Fishing article, indicate bullet weight, which is an important element in cartridge performance. While it is tempting to assume the bullet was 130 grains, which became the standard weight for this cartridge

later on, that might not have been the case with the initial introduction of the round in 1900.

A U.S. Government report of the War Department for the fiscal year 1900 includes a test report of automatic pistols. It tested the Colt Model 1900 pistol in caliber .38 Automatic (six-inch barrel) in early 1900 with a velocity (at 53 feet) of 1,259 fps. However, the cartridge had a 105-grain metal jacketed bullet, not a 130-grain bullet. It had a charge weight of 7.8 grains of smokeless powder. The report also mentions the use of a second lot of ammunition with a lower velocity of 935 fps. That report does not indicate its bullet weight, but it did predict that it might not cycle the gun reliably, since it had much lower velocity. Of the 350 rounds of this second ammunition fired, it was reported there were two instances where the "sliding cover [slide?] did not recoil to its full extent." Does this imply that it had the same bullet weight? One can only speculate.

It's not known if the 107-grain load is the same round that Sheldon and the *Shooting and Fishing* article refer to, but the velocity is the same.

The 1904 Thompson-LaGarde Report lists two loads for the .38 Automatic ammunition used in their tests with a Colt Military Model 1902 (six-inch barrel): a 130-grain jacketed bullet at 1,107 fps, and a 120-grain soft-point at 1,048 fps. The 130-grain round had a charge weight of 6.6 grains of smokeless powder, while the 120-grain round had a charge weight of 6.5 grains. Thus it can be see that, between 1900 and 1904, there was considerable variation in the bullet weights and velocities of the .38 Automatic cartridge.

Another source, published nearly a decade before the introduction of the Colt Super .38 pistol, showed another range of velocities for the .38 Automatic. Captain H.B.C. Pollard's 1920 book lists

AUTOMATIC COLT PISTOL.

(Browning's Patent.)

38 CALIBRE.

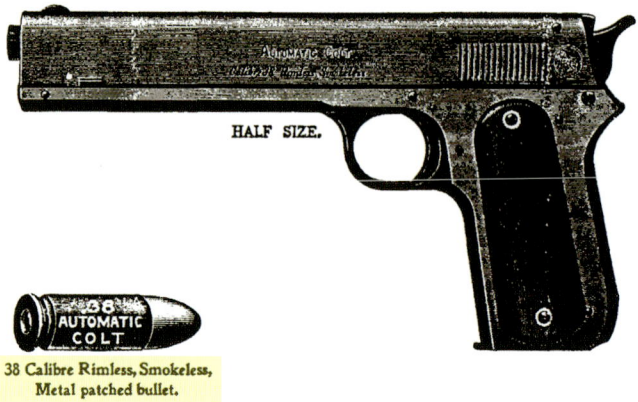

HALF SIZE.

38 Calibre Rimless, Smokeless,
Metal patched bullet.

Capacity of magazine, 7 shots.

THE action of this pistol is automatic except that the trigger is pulled for firing each shot. The arm can be discharged at the rate of 5 shots per second, the cartridges being automatically supplied from a detachable magazine inserted in the handle of the pistol.

After the pistol is charged with a filled magazine, one opening movement is made by hand, bringing the first cartridge into the chamber. On pulling the trigger the cartridge is fired, the empty shell is extracted, a new cartridge is loaded into the chamber, all these operations taking place automatically without any manipulation of the arm. This automatic operation of the pistol is effected by the recoil of the moving parts, and as a consequence, the recoil is so absorbed in being utilized that it has not the usual disturbing effect.

Length of Barrel,	-	-	6 inches.
Length of Pistol over all,	-		9 inches.
Weight of Pistol,	-	-	35 ounces.

Made only in the .38 calibre with 6 inch barrel, blued finish.

COLT'S PATENT FIRE ARMS MANUFACTURING CO.

425 and 427 Market Street,   HARTFORD.   26 Glasshouse Street,
   San Francisco, Cal.   CONN.   London W. England.

Fig. 3: Colt's Model 1900 Pistol

Colt "Super .38" Automatic Pistol

CALIBER .38

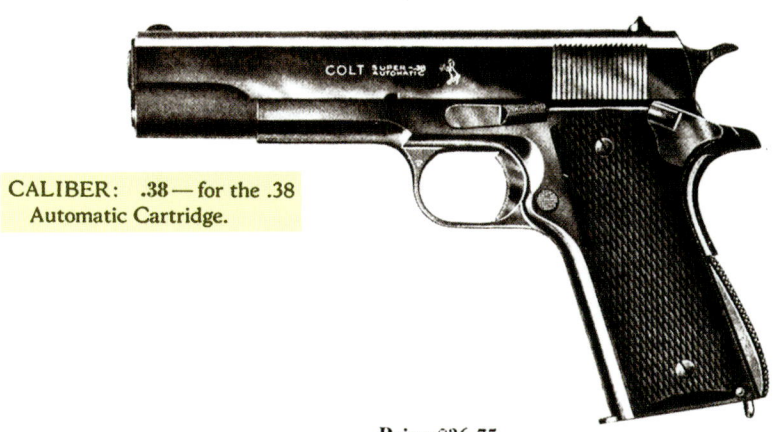

CALIBER: .38 — for the .38 Automatic Cartridge.

Price $36.75

Colt Checked Arched Housing.

The Colt .45 Automatic as well as the Super .38 and ACE Automatic Pistols are fitted with checked arched housings, providing a full, firm grip that makes slipping impossible. The built out housing snugly fits the palm of the hand, aiding in steadying the arm, as well as making the grip more comfortable and more secure. The Colt checked arched housing is found only in Colt Automatic Pistols.

General Specifications

CAPACITY OF MAGAZINE: 9 Cartridges.

LENGTH OF BARREL: 5 inches.

LENGTH OVER ALL: 8½ inches.

STOCKS: Checked Walnut.

TRIGGER: Checked.

ARCHED HOUSING: Checked.

FINISH: Full Blued.

WEIGHT: 39 ounces.

Modeled after that most famous of all Automatic Pistols — the Colt Government Model .45 — this new Super .38 bids fair to match its famous brother in all that a well made powerful Arm can do. It has every merit a Gun could possibly possess — backed by over 94 years' experience of the oldest and most famous manufacturer of Fire Arms in the world — makers of Colts since 1836. A grip that is certain, an action that is positive and Safety Locks that simply cannot fail — every outstanding feature of the already proven Colt .45 Automatic is embodied in this new Super .38, and to them has been added the distinct advantage of the .38 caliber automatic cartridge with its exceptionally high velocity.

Special Features

The new Colt Super .38 Automatic Pistol will be hailed with unstinted appreciation by the Hunter of Big Game, the Trapper, the Explorer and Target Shooter. Thoroughly tested in the hands of those who recognize a perfect Fire Arm, the new Colt Super .38 Automatic Pistol has shown an enviable record of results.

With the one exception of caliber, the Colt Super .38 is identical in construction with the Colt .45 Government Model. It is equipped with both manual and automatic Safety Locks exactly the same as the .45 — the Arched Housing, extension horn on grip and quick magazine release.

.38 AUTOMATIC

Fig. 4: Colt's 1932 Catalog

published velocities of 1,175 fps (Winchester; from a six-inch barrel), 1,000 fps (Kynoch, barrel length unreported) for a 130-grain bullet, and 1,100 fps for a 128-grain bullet (Ely, barrel length unreported).

Major J.S. Hatcher wrote a review of the new Colt pistol that was published in the May 1929 issue of *The American Rifleman* (*reproduced in Sheldon, 1997*). Major Hatcher speaks only of the .38 Automatic cartridge. He does not mention anything about a new cartridge or new loadings of the .38 Automatic. His velocity listings for the 13-grain .38 ACP are 1,190, 1,150, 1,126, and 1,080 fps from different makers (not identified).

Major Hatcher piles heaps of praise on the .38 Automatic cartridge, which he also refers to as the .38 Military (this name is derived from the Model 1902 .38 Military pistol). In fact, Major Hatcher talks about the cartridge for almost two full pages of the three-page article. He notes that its exceptional velocity and power is far superior to anything else that exists at the time, including the 9mm Luger. He emphasizes that the cartridge has been around for quite some time, with no reference to any new loadings.

These reports show that the velocities and bullet weights of the .38 Automatic covered a wide range prior to when Colt introduced the new Super .38 pistol.

Sheldon (*1997*) continues that the .38 Automatic cartridge velocity was "... increased to 1,300 fps sometime in late 1932*, initially by Remington Arms Company when they developed a new line of high speed oil proof handgun cartridges. This is where the confusion begins, since it is unknown if and when all other cartridge manufacturers followed suit and also increased the velocity of their .38 auto cartridges."

The ad in Sheldon's book that shows the first mention of the velocity increase

in 1932/1933 to 1,300 fps described it as, " ... the New Super .38 Cartridge ... ." At the same time, the text in the article reads that the gun is "chambered to shoot the powerful, high velocity .38 Automatic cartridge." The .38 Super name for the cartridge didn't catch on in Colt's ads for quite some time, even if it was recognized as a new loading in 1932/1933.

Table 1: Advertised velocities of the .38 Automatic ammunition in Colt's ads with a 130-grain bullet from 1928 through 1933.

Colt's continued to advertise that its Super .38 pistol was chambered for the .38 Automatic cartridge well into the 1940s, though you'll note that it refers to both the .38 Automatic and Super .38 cartridges in the 1941 catalog.

(Fig. 5) At some point, the name of the cartridge was changed to .38 Super Automatic, though it's not known when individual ammunition manufacturers did so. A reprint of Colt's 1957 catalog does list the ammunition for the Super .38 pistol as .38 Super Automatic.

(Fig. 6) Eventually, .38 Super Automatic ammunition started to lose speed. The 1957 Colt's catalog still shows a velocity of 1,300 fps, but a 1969 Colt's product sheet lists a velocity of 1,280 fps for the 130-grain bullet (*Sheldon, 1997*). The speed has dropped since then. Current published velocities for the same bullet are 1,215 fps (Winchester, Remington) and 1,200 fps (Federal).

News of a new cartridge or a new load is usually pointed out with great zeal. Yet nothing in the ads for the first few years say anything about the birth of a new cartridge, since it is consistently referred to by its old name. It wasn't until 1932/1933 that Remington increased the velocity to 1,300 fps, and this was adver-

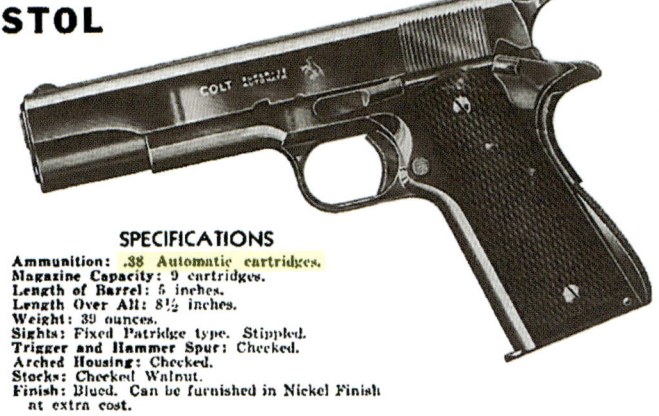

SUPER .38 AUTOMATIC PISTOL

CALIBER: .38

For the big game hunter, and the lover of the outdoors, the Super .38 offers an arm of unsurpassed power and efficiency. It is built on the same frame as the Government Model and has all of the safety features found in this famous gun. It is especially popular because of the powerful Super .38 cartridges which it handles — having a muzzle velocity of approximately 1,300 foot seconds. Will stop any animal on the American continent and is a favorite for use as an auxiliary arm for big game hunting. Magazine holds 9 cartridges.

SPECIFICATIONS

Ammunition: .38 Automatic cartridges.
Magazine Capacity: 9 cartridges.
Length of Barrel: 5 inches.
Length Over All: 8½ inches.
Weight: 39 ounces.
Sights: Fixed Patridge type. Stippled.
Trigger and Hammer Spur: Checked.
Arched Housing: Checked.
Stocks: Checked Walnut.
Finish: Blued. Can be furnished in Nickel Finish at extra cost.

Fig. 5: Colt's 1941 Catalog

tised widely at the time, just like it would be today. Even so, the cartridge name remained the same in Colt's ads and catalogs until the 1940s/1950s, when the name .38 Super Automatic appears to be consistently applied to the ammunition.

Interestingly, there was some confusion about what ammunition was appropriate for the older pre-1929 .38 Automatic pistols, up until the 1940s. Sheldon (*1997*) reprints correspondence between Colt's Manufacturing Company and Western Cartridge Company dated December 8, 1944, to clarify which ammunition is safe for which gun. Excerpts from this letter read:

Some years ago ... it was decided that the Super .38 cartridge as a load, having a velocity of about 1,300 f.s [sic] was perfectly safe in the Super .38 Automatic Pistol and the older type .38 caliber pistols, known as the Pocket Model [1903] and Military Model [1902]. In fact, Remington Arms Company published such a statement on their Super .38 cartridge boxes for some time.

Later, in going more carefully into the characteristics of the Super .38 cartridge, and also in checking the design of the

two older automatic pistol models, it was felt wise to recommend the Super .38 cartridge only for the Super .38 Pistol. As a result, a cartridge with lower velocity was brought out by some of the companies and this is the cartridge that we have recommended for use in the two older models. We do not recommend the present Super .38 cartridge with its muzzle velocity of about 1,300 f.s., for use in the two older models.

Follow-up correspondence from Western Cartridge Company to Remington Arms Company dated December 18, 1944, also reproduced in Sheldon (*1997*) reads:

This is the first indication we have had from the Colt Company on the reversal of their policy that the 1,300 f.s. velocity cartridge is suitable for firing in older models.

The letter continues with a quote of what was supposedly written on the Remington ammunition box (ammunition which Western Cartridge Company indicates it received December 21, 1936). Interestingly, this is a quote attributed to Colt. The quote reads:

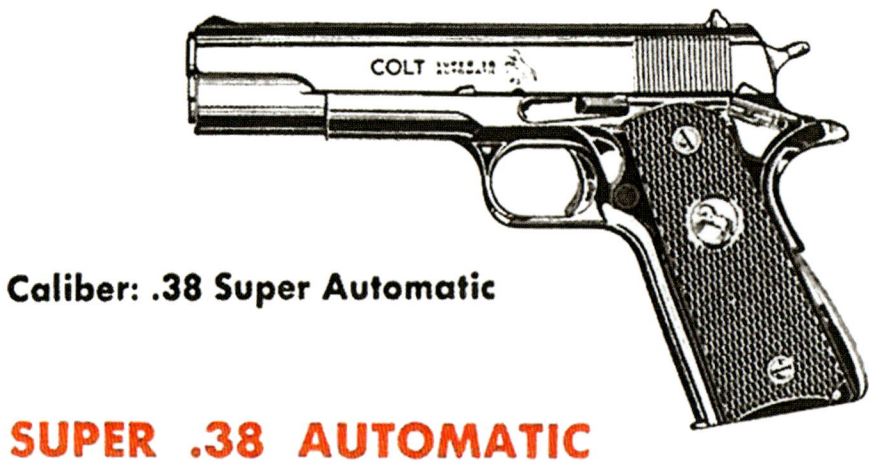

Caliber: .38 Super Automatic

SUPER .38 AUTOMATIC

This powerful handgun has all of the construction features of the world-famous Colt Government Model .45 plus the distinct advantage of the .38 caliber automatic cartridge with its exceptionally high velocity of 1300 foot seconds.

AMMUNITION: .38 Super Automatic.
MAGAZINE CAPACITY: 9 rounds.
LENGTH OF BARREL: 5".
LENGTH OVERALL: 8½".
WEIGHT: 39 oz.
SIGHTS: Fixed type, ramp-style, glare-proofed.
ARCHED HOUSING.
TRIGGER: Grooved.
HAMMER SPUR: Grooved.
STOCKS: Checkered Coltwood.
FINISH: Colt Blue or Nickel.

Retail Price: **$78.25** Blue
$86.10 Nickel

Shipping Weight: 3¼ lbs.

Fig. 6: Colt's 1957 Catalog

These cartridges are specifically designed for the Super .38 Automatic Colt and can be used in Automatic Colt caliber .38 of earlier design. We strongly recommend them for use in these arms.—Colt's Patent Fire Arms Mfg. Co.

This correspondence indicates that it was not the conventional wisdom we accept today, that the only round for the older pre-1929 models was a load of no more than approximately1,050 fps with a 130-grain bullet. For some years after the Colt Super .38 pistol was introduced in 1929, the souped-up .38 Automatic ammunition was thought safe by Colt itself for the pre-1929 pistols. Only later was this view reversed.

We now recognize two separate loadings for these cartridges. A low-pressure (26,500 psi) .38 Automatic and a high pressure (36,500 psi) .38 Super Automatic. The official name for the .38 Super Automatic is the .38 Super Automatic +P. The +P designation was added to the .38 Super Automatic name, in 1974 (Speer Reloading Manual, 2007), to help distin-

sion 1/11/2013), list the nominal velocity for the .38 Super Automatic +P with a 130-grain bullet as 1,200 fps. Yes, it has been loaded down from its once impressive 1,300 fps. The current .38 Automatic has also been reduced from its heyday. Its nominal velocity is 1,035 fps with the same bullet and is intended for the older pre-1929 guns.

NICKEL CASES

Sometime in the 1930s, some manufacturers started to use nickel plated cases for their .38 Super Automatic loads (*Sheldon, 1997*). I ran across some older ammunition for the .38 Automatic in both brass and nickel and chronographed them through a Colt Government Model. None of these rounds were in their original boxes, so they can't be dated, and none of the bullets were weighed. Still, the brass-cased ammunition was at a lower velocity than the nickel-plated cases (shown in theTable), and, in most of these examples, the nickel-plated cases had the name "Super" in their headstamps. However, the name Super

This Remington-UMC .38 Automatic round is an example. It might have come from a box labeled .38 Super Automatic, but that's not known, nor is its intended velocity. These rounds chronographed an average of 1,212 fps.

VINTAGE .38 AUTOMATIC AMMUNITION

(Fig. 7) I obtained an old box of .38 Automatic ammunition that dates from 1916-1919, according to a guide found at http://cartridgecollectors.org. This ammunition would be from 93 to 96 years old at the time of the test (November 2012). The box did not have its original factory seal, so I can't verify that the ammunition was true to that era. It had a full complement of 50 rounds, all with the same brass/bullet. The brass was marked "REM-UMC 38 ACP" with a "U" stamped on the primer. The bullets were cupronickel jacketed. Some cases and bullets had corrosion.

(Fig. 8) I pulled three bullets. Their diameter was not uniformly circular. The diameters were: 1) .356- to .360-inch; 2) .357- to .358-inch; and 3)

Fig. 7

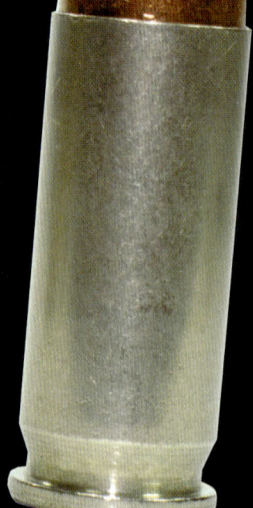

.357- to .359-inch. Bullet weights were 131.7, 130.6, 130.7 grains. The small, flake-type gunpowder charge weighed an average of 4.8 grains.

I tried to fire 10 rounds over a chronograph. Six rounds fired, four were duds and would not fire after 10 hits with the firing pin. The primer was very hard and the firing pin produced only a shallow dent on the first hit; the test gun had a 19-pound mainspring. Their hardness might have been due to age. Of the six rounds that fired, one went off with the first firing pin hit, four required two hits, and one required five hits. Three of the rounds were hangfires, with the longest hangfire less than a ½-second.

Velocity spread was from 1,002 to 1,065 fps from a five-inch Kart barrel, with an average of 1,028 fps. The typical velocity gain/loss per inch runs between 25 and 50 fps, so these would run a bit faster from the six-inch barrel of Colt's 1900-1902 model guns of that era. The published velocity for this ammunition is unknown.

Firing ammunition this old is not recommended, and this is not an endorsement to do so.

SUMMARY

There was no new cartridge introduced in 1929 called the .38 Super Automatic with the introduction of Colt's Super .38 Automatic pistol. Colt's advertisements and catalogs from that period clearly show that the new gun was chambered for the old .38 Automatic. It took four to five years (December 1928 to December 1932/1933), until the velocity of the 38 Automatic was increased from 1,190 fps to 1,300 fps. Only then was the cartridge referred to as the "New Super .38 Cartridge" (*Sheldon, 1997*). This eventually morphed into the name .38 Super, though it's uncertain when that name made it onto cartridge boxes or the

Fig. 8

cartridges themselves.

The evidence supports Sheldon (*1997*) in that there was no increase in velocity with the introduction of the new Colt pistol, since velocities with 130-grain bullets were similar to those that appear to be common at the time. Major Hatcher's 1929 article mentions no new loadings for the .38 Automatic and gives the impression that the rounds he tested

and offer high performance. Check out products from Buffalo Bore, CorBon, DoubleTap, Underwood Ammunition, and Wilson Combat, to name a few.

About the Author: *Brad Miller was raised in Idaho. He attended Idaho State University, earning a B.S. in Psychology, in 1984, then a graduate degree from Cornell University, and, eventually, a Ph.D. in Biopsychology, in 1991. He has been a shooting enthusiast for more than 40 years and has handloaded more than 100,000 rounds. Most have been fired through 1911-type pistols, his favorite projectile delivery platform.*

Miller began amateur gunsmithing on the 1911 pistol, in the 1990s. He attended a class on accurizing the 1911 pistol in Trinidad, Colorado, in 1997, that class taught by Jim Stroh, owner of Alpha Precision, in Comer, Georgia. Since then, he has custom-built about a dozen 1911s, including Colt, Springfield Armory, Caspian, STI,

Para-Ordnance, in .45 ACP, .38 Super, 9x23 Winchester, 9mm Luger, and .40 S&W.

Miller began competitive shooting in the 1970s. He has participated in PPC, rifle and pistol silhouette, DCM, IDPA,

COLT'S PROMOTION OF THE SUPER .38 PISTOL

Colt's advertisements might seem a little comical by today's standards. It advertised the new pistol with the .38 Automatic cartridge, "Will stop any animal on the American Continent." Images of bobcats, bears, mountain lions, and moose often decorated the ads.

Here are some examples of advertisements used to describe the Colt Super .38 pistol and ammunition from Sheldon's 1997 book and Colt's catalogs.

- "The Ideal "One-hand-gun" for Big Game. Will stop any animal on the American Continent. The .38 Automatic Colt Cartridge has high velocity and flat trajectory, great shocking power and deep penetration." The American Rifleman, December 1928.
- "A Real He-Man Gun." 1929 through ??
- "The .38 Colt Automatic cartridge, unsurpassed in power and 1190 feet per second velocity, is here given its due in an arm that bids fair to set new records, on the range, in the woods ... as well as in popularity." National Sportsman, August 1929.
- "Ideal for Big Game – and Target Shooting." The American Rifleman, May 1929.
- "No arm of similar caliber has even enjoyed such an enthusiastic reception from Shooters, Hunters, Guides, Explorers and others who appreciate an arm of superior workmanship, absolute accuracy, and unusual shocking power, as has been accorded the new Colt Super .38 Automatic." The American Rifleman, May 1930.
- "No animal on the American continent can resist the tremendous shocking power of its swift-traveling, hard-hitting bullet with a muzzle velocity of approximately 1,200 foot seconds." National Sportsman, March 1931.
- "Stopped in its tracks!" Along with a drawing of a bear. 1930s.
- "Super-powered for BIG GAME HUNTING." Includes drawings of a bear and moose. 1930s.
- "No wonder the Colt Super .38 is the favorite arm of trappers, explorers and big game hunters everywhere! This rugged, hard hitting gun stops deer, bear and mountain lion ... swiftly, surely, eagerly. No game on the American continent can compete with its super-powered wallop, its unfailing accuracy." Unknown publication, middle to late 1930s (Sheldon, 1997).
- " ... the Super .38 offers an arms of unsurpassed power and efficiency." October 1941 Colt catalog.
- "Has a Whack like a pile driver." "It's a super-powered, accurate big game automatic that can stop anything on the American continent." "Deals a wicked wallop." Includes a photo of a dead moose. National Sportsman ad. Date unknown.
- "Police and Sheriff's are showing keen interest in the Colt Super .38 – due to its hard-hitting power, its fast action and its large capacity magazine. For riot cars, special duty and mounted service, you can't beat the Super .38 Automatic. The Super .38 shoots an unusually powerful cartridge and its bullet will go through gas tanks and automobile bodies like nothing at all." Date unknown.

FOOTNOTES & REFRENCES

*There is a minor discrepancy here. Sheldon writes that it was 1932, but he refers to the ad in which the first mention of 1,300 fps appears as published in December of 1933.

[1] The following is a list of publications, articles and resources stating the .38 Super Automatic cartridge was created in 1929. This is not intended to be a complete list. Other articles that make this claim likely exist since this has been the mantra on the origin of the cartridge for quite some time. This is simply a list of sources that the author has casually come across over recent years.

Barnes, F.C. 2006. *Cartridges Of The World, 11th Edition,* Edited by S. Skinner, Gun Digest Books, Iola, WI.

7th Edition Hornady Handbook of Cartridge Reloading. 2007. Hornady Manufacturing Company, Grand Island, NE.

Speer Reloading Manual #14. 2007. Ed. Allan Jones. ATK/Speer, Lewiston, ID.

Sierra Rifle & Handgun Reloading Data Edition V, 4th printing. 2003.

Lyman Third Edition Pistol & Revolver Handbook. 2004. T.J. Griffin, editor. Lyman Products Corporation, Middletown, CT.

Charles E. Petty, 2000. "Reloading for the .38 Super Auto." *American Rifleman*, November/December. pp. 38-42. Note: The article shows an old era ad indicating the cartridge name as .38 Automatic with a velocity of 1190, but Petty claims the name of the cartridge is .38 Super Auto and it was a "new" loading.

Stan Trzoniec, 2003. "Kimber .38 Super." *Handloader*, February-March, pp. 22-26.

http://www.firearmsforum.com/firearms/article/2948

http://www.americanrifleman.org/articles/the-super-38/

Richard Mann, 2012. "True pair: Making the case for 38 Super +P." *American Rifleman*, November. pp. 66-69; 110-111. An electronic version can be found at: http://www.americanrifleman.org/articles/making-the-case-for-38-super-plus-p/

References

Annual Reports of the War Department for the Fiscal Year ended June 30, 1900. Report of the Chief of Ordnance. Washington, Government printing office. A copy of this report can be seen at this location on the internet: http://books.google.com/books?id=ajY-AQAAMAAJ&printsec=frontcover#v=onepage&q&f=false

ANSI/SAAMI booklet Z299.3-1993. American National Standard. Voluntary Industry Performance Standards for Pressure and Velocity of Centerfire Pistol and Revolver Ammunition for the Use of Commercial Manufacturers. 1993. Sporting Arms & Ammunition Manufacturers' Institute, Inc., Wilton, Conn. USA. PDF versions of the SAAMI publications are available on the internet at: http://www.saami.org/

Colt .38 Automatic Pistols 1900-1911 Models. Date unknown. Reprinted by Cornell publications.

Colt Revolvers and Automatic Pistols, (Colt's, The Arm of Law and Order) 1929 catalog. Colt's Patent Fire Arms Manufacturing Co. Small Arms Division, Hartford, Conn., U.S.A. Reprinted by Cornell Publications.

Colt Revolvers and Automatic Pistols, July 1932 catalog. Colt's Patent Fire Arms Manufacturing Co. Small Arms Division, Hartford, Conn., U.S.A. (Original catalog.)

Colt Revolvers and Automatic Pistols, October 1941 catalog. Colt's Patent Fire Arms Manufacturing Co., Small Arms Division, Hartford, Connecticut. Reprinted by Cornell Publications.

Colt Revolvers and Automatic Pistols, February 1957 catalog. Colt's Patent Fire Arms Manufacturing Co. Inc., Hartford 15, Conn. Reprinted by Cornell Publications.

Haven, C.T. and Belden, F. A. 1940. *The History of the Colt Revolver.* Bonanza Books, New York.

Permanent International Commission for Firearms Testing – abbreviated as C.I.P. or CIP. (Commission internationale permanente pour l'épreuve des armes à feu portatives.) On the internet at: http://www.cip-

CHAPTER 22

HANDLOADING FOR THE 1911

BY PHILIP P. MASSARO, PRESIDENT/OWNER
MASSARO BALLISTIC LABORATORIES

THE TRENCHES OF FRANCE, the shores of Iwo Jima, Saipan, Anzio, Juno, Sword, the Tet Offensive. All those battles conjure images of brave soldiers putting their lives on the line, with one common denominator, regardless the decade: the 1911 on their hip.

Designed by the gifted John Moses Browning in 1905 for military use, the revolutionary pistol destined to be renamed the M1911 and adopted by the U.S. Military used a relatively new concept in cartridge design. The straight-walled case was designed with neither rim nor shoulder to give positive headspacing. Instead, it was designed to use the tiny case mouth for headspacing. Its relatively small case generated enough energy to operate the autoloading mechanism around which the pistol was built.

Our soldiers had reported the detriments of the .38 Long Colt cartridges in a sidearm, when used in the Philippines during their little problem there in the very early 1900s. In simple words, the enemy had to be shot more than once, and that's not a good thing. Our soldiers needed and deserved something new and better. Military designers had settled on the idea that no lesser bore diameter had the stopping power of the .452-inch bullets, a size proven on the battlefields of the western U.S. in the 1870s and 1880s. However, the single-action revolvers chambered for the .45 Colt were cumbersome to carry and slow to reload in the heat of battle. The Browning design presented by Colt's solved that problem. It fired a 200-grain .45-caliber bullet at roughly 900 fps, from a slim, magazine-fed pistol that could withstand the rigors of

A good set of dies is important

battle and consistently deliver the goods. Its performance was just shy of the Cavalry favored .45 Colt, and proved itself early on in The Great War, throughout Europe. Mr. Browning's brainchild, the .45 ACP (Automatic Colt Pistol), would be the standard issue sidearm cartridge until the 1990s, seeing duty in the First and Second World Wars, the Korean War, and the Vietnam conflict. The military had modified John Browning's original choice of a 200-grain bullet, settling on a 230-grain round-nose bullet traveling at 800 fps. This design fed very well from the spring-loaded magazine and provided the knock down power our soldiers needed.

My Dad, ol' Grumpy Pants (GP), inherited a WWII-era 1911 from an older colleague. This gun had seen duty in the Pacific theater and was fitted with a nice pair of elk horn grips after the war, but that was the only modification. The gun had not been, well, "maintained." When GP handed the gun to me, first to clean it for him and second to take it out to our backyard range, I immediately noticed the rough condition of the barrel. Even after a thorough cleaning, it sort of looked like a rusty culvert pipe. The box of 1943 vintage ball ammunition didn't exactly fill me with confidence, either. I questioned the stability of the primers after 60 years.

I soon found out I had nothing to worry about. As a matter of fact, my pal Josh Coon came out to the range with me, toting his brand new Springfield

Armory 1911 and a new box of fancy Federal ammunition. Well, not only did GP's pistol shoot well, it outshot the new Springfield. This is no slight to Springfield's product, which is an amazing pistol, but it is a testament to the timeless construction of the 1911. Even after all that time (and neglect), and with a less than pristine barrel, it fired very well, with no jams and damned fine accuracy. Let's just say it made a believer and a convert out of me very quickly. The 1911 in .45ACP is a great combination, one that's stood the test of time. Certainly, this cartridge isn't going away any time soon.

It certainly isn't a cartridge that has the look of power and reach. Quite honestly, its profile resembles that of Danny DeVito. However, in that short, round-headed package, it gave the U.S. soldier a tool that proved quite effective in combat; few cartridges of lesser caliber possess the .45 ACP's knockdown power. One of the beauties of the .45ACP is that its low velocities are easy on the hands and easier on the ears. Most loads are subsonic, which makes it a great round for recreational shooting. It isn't a powder hog either, with almost all loads staying between five and 10 grains of powder. This equals 700 to 1,400 shots to the pound of powder—very economical!

The .45 ACP has the same case head dimensions as the 7x57 Mauser, .30-06 Springfield, and .308 Winchester, as the military usually desires continuity for a minimum of tooling costs. This rimless design allows for great extraction upon firing.

As I mentioned, the cartridge headspaces off of the case mouth. What this means for handloaders is that you must be certain *not* to use a roll crimp when creating your ammunition, as it will deform the case mouth and, thereby, affect the headspacing. A taper crimp, instead, will keep your bullets comfortably nestled in the case, while leaving the case mouth intact. Lee and other companies make a special taper crimp die that will easily provide the proper level of crimp.

I generally prefer a tungsten carbide die set for my .45 work, as the cases won't need to be lubricated. RCBS, Lee, Redding, and Hornady all offer high-quality die sets, including a die to flare the case mouth. Set up your dies for full-length resizing, to guarantee good feeding with your 1911. While flaring the case mouth, only flare as much as you need to properly seat the bullets. Over-flaring the case mouth will result in shorter case life, as the brass gets overworked and becomes brittle prematurely. Five, six, or seven firings are not unheard of in this low pressure case.

Most .45 ACP cases use a Large Pistol primer (we'll get into this in more detail in a moment), and a relatively light powder charge. Care must be taken when loading these cases to avoid a double charge of powder, as the case has the capacity to hold that much. Of course, that would create extremely dangerous pressures. I've seen handguns literally blown in half from the accidental double charge.

For powder choice, I generally prefer Alliant's Blue Dot for the heavier bullets and Alliant's Unique for the lighter projectiles. They give a good balance of safe pressures and good velocities. Unique tends to burn on the dirty side, but man, it is wonderfully accurate. Hodgdon's TiteGroup is a powder that gives the same velocities as other powders, yet with a lighter charge. It makes a good choice for those on a tight budget, as its name suggests.

There's a very wide choice of bullets available to the handloader. The 1911 shooter who wishes to use their pistol for self-defense has some great choices at their disposal. Hornady's XTP features a heavy jacket, to control expansion, and it is a very accurate bullet. The Speer Gold Dot is a bonded core bullet designed for deep penetration. Sierra offers the SportsMaster jacketed hollowpoint bullet and, like most of its products, they are a very well-made bullet suitable for a self-defense round. Cutting Edge Bullets offers an all-copper hollowpoint bullet for the .45 ACP that has a very deep cavity. Upon impact, the bullet is designed to expand, causing the frontal portion to separate into four "petals," while still driving the solid rear portion deep into the target. I like this design! They are offered in weights from 150 grains up to 240 grains in .45-caliber. The wound channels from these types of bullets should prove sufficient enough to combat the zombie hoards and other plagues of the undead, while keeping your anatomy in its current configuration.

For the target shooter or for use in the gun games, cast lead bullets make an affordable choice. You can cast your own from a healthy supply of lead, with some wheel weights mixed in for hardness, and there are companies like Falcon Bullets that offer very consistent hard-cast bullets as components for the handloader. The 185-grain semi-wadcutter makes a great light load for the gun games and for plinking. Velocities can be held to the same 800 fps as the heavier bullets, but with less recoil, for quicker target acquisition on the follow-up shots. These bullets usually feed very well in the 1911

platform, if the feed ramp is nicely polished.

Falcon also makes a great 230-grain round-nose hard-cast bullet, made to match the profile of the original 230-grain FMJ military issue projectile. I've had very good results with this bullet and 5.0 grains of Hodgdon's Tite-Group powder.

For those using the indoor shooting ranges, where exposed lead can create a dangerous level of lead vapor, a fully encapsulated bullet makes a wise and often necessary choice. Rainier Ballistics makes this type of bullet, in 185-, 200- and 230-grain weights. These include flat-points, hollowpoints, semi-wadcutters, and FMJ configurations. All these bullets are completely encased in copper, almost eliminating the risk of vaporized lead in the air upon firing.

Speaking of the indoor ranges and exposed lead, I must warn you that there are some .45 ACP cases that feature a Small Pistol primer pocket. My understanding is that these came into existence to utilize the lead-free Small Pistol primers on the market, and they are recommended for use at the indoor ranges. To accommodate this lead-free theme, some companies produce .45ACP cases with the Small pocket dimension and these unleaded primers. For us handloaders, the loading data doesn't change, but there is an inherent risk in reloading these cases. If you confuse the two primers sizes and you try to squeeze a Large Pistol primer into a Small primer pocket, there is a risk of primer detonation. This is a bad enough scenario, if you're using a hand primer, as the risk of injury is present, but in a progressive press where a multitude of primers and powder are contained in the same unit, it

can be a recipe for disaster. Be very sure to inspect and segregate all your .45 ACP cases and keep the Small primer pocket variety in a different location altogether.

As a hunting round, the .45 ACP with its lighter bullet weights and its moderate velocities are useful on varmints, but I don't think it makes a good choice for deer-sized game. The energies generated are just too low to ensure a quick kill. That said, there is another cartridge that is offered in the 1911 platform that does make a decent hunting round: the 10mm Auto. It offers a .400-inch diameter bullet at velocities just a couple hundred fps shy of the performance of the .41 Remington Magnum. Bullet weights range from 155 grains through 200 grains, and velocities are in the neighborhood

of 1,300 fps and 1,200 fps, respectively. Now we're cooking with gas!

As you've read in previous chapters, the 10mm case began life on the drawing board of renowned firearms expert and U.S. Marine Col. Jeff Cooper and came to be adopted by the FBI after a shootout with bank robbers in Florida, showed the lack of stopping power of the Bureau-issued .38 Special and 9mm Luger handguns. The two suspects in this particular case were shot six and 12 times, respectively, before they were killed. Seven agents were killed or wounded by the two shooters, and the FBI laid a portion of the blame on the handguns the agents were carrying. You can now imagine why the hunt for a heavier, more powerful cartridge was

The low pressure nature of .45 ACP makes it a very forgiving cartridge to reload.

Bayou Bullet uses an amazing coating.

on. The 10mm Auto got the nod initially, but the sharp recoil of the Big 10 was too much for some investigators to handle effectively.

The 10mm operates at a much higher pressure level and velocity than the .45ACP and its recoil ramps up accordingly. But, at these performance levels, the 10mm Auto has the capability of being a suitable hunting round. Were I to use the cartridge for hunting, I'd probably opt for something along the lines of a 180-grain Hornady XTP or, perhaps, a Nosler Sporting Handgun 200-grain bullet at a velocity of 1,200 fps. This should handily convert deer and hogs into venison and bacon.

The 10mm Auto also makes a very good choice in self-defense rounds. It does recoil harder than the .45ACP, but it is still manageable. Bullets like the 155-grain Speer Gold Dot would serve well to save your derrière. Muzzle flash and jump can be on the heavy side (just ask Mr. Loëb, who lit up the night sky in Texas), but, with some practice, you can become very proficient with your pistol. One of my favorite loads with that 155-grain Speer bullet is 11.5 grains of Blue Dot, with a Winchester WLP primer. It has plenty of velocity and is quite impressive in the accuracy department. There are hard-cast lead bullets in .400-inch diameter available as well, which are great for practice rounds and plinking. Be sure to choose a nose profile that will feed well in your 10mm, to avoid the possibility of a jam.

Like the venerable .45ACP, both Blue Dot and Unique powders work well in this case, as well as Accurate Arms No. 9. The 10mm Auto also uses the Large Pistol primers, but read your reloading manual carefully, as some loads are tested and developed with Large Pistol Magnum primers, needing a hotter spark to ignite the bigger charges of powder.

That recoil factor of full-house 10mm Auto loads I have mentioned earlier resulted in the necessary reduction of the Big 10's velocity to subsonic levels, to make the 10mm usable by agents of all shapes and statures. Realizing that the reduced loading left quite a bit of room in the case, the firm of Smith & Wesson shortened the case to hold a charge that would give just under 1,000 fps with a 180-grain 10mm bullet. Alas, the .40 S&W was born. The 10mm Auto fans often mock the shorter case, referring to it the .40 Short & Weak. However, the .40 S&W makes a great defense round in a compact 1911 rig, with bullet weight falling between the 9mms and the .45s. It is a common choice of law enforcement departments, as it possesses the desired knockdown power, while allowing the officer to carry more ammunition. That alone should be a good endorsement for the .40 S&W. It is based on the 10mm Auto case, shortened from 0.992-inch to 0.850-inch and uses a Small Pistol primer instead of the 10mm's Large. Among common pistol propellants, Blue Dot, Power Pistol, Unique, and Tite Group all work well in this case. I like the heavier 165- and 180-grain jacketed bullets, and Falcon makes a hard-cast 180-grain, truncated cone, flat-point bullet that makes a fine choice for practice. The love affair between law enforcement and the .40 S&W will ensure good supplies

of brass and bullets will be available for years to come.

Now, if you like the 9mm bore diameter in a 1911 pistol, the .38 Super also makes a good handgun. This is an improvement of the classic .38 ACP cartridge, designed to operate at a much higher pressure level than its venerable predecessor (see the sidebar by Brad Miller in the previous chapter).

Although the velocities attainable by the handloader don't always make it a viable choice for the USPSA Major power factor, it still is a fun gun to own and use. The heavier 147-grain bullets can be pushed to about 1,100fps, which isn't all that far off .357 Magnum velocities. It does this with much less powder than the .357 uses. Accurate Arms No. 9 ranks among the powders that give the best velocities. Couple this with a quality Small Pistol primer and you should have a nice, compact handgun capable of great accuracy. The .38 Super was initially designed to headspace off the semi-rim, but that has been changed on most modern guns to headspace off the case mouth, like the .45ACP.

As a self-defense cartridge, I personally feel the 9mm/.358-inch diameter bullets fall short of the performance of the .40s and .45s, but, if the ranges are close, this chambering can suffice as well as the .38 Specials and .357 Magnums that we have relied on for decades. Handgun guru Elmer Keith (please bow your heads), was impressed with the .38 Super's ability to penetrate the bulletproof vests of his day, and the FBI used this round, albeit briefly, during J. Edgar Hoover's era. As a hunting gun, the .38 Super might suffice on deer-sized game, although there are better tools for the job. Colt marketed this round as a suitable choice for all big game, when it was released, but I'm not so sure about that!

When developing a load for your 1911, always start at the lowest load and work up slowly, watching for pressure signs and making sure your ammunition feeds properly from the magazine, with no jams. The usual loading techniques apply, but some attention to detail will make the autoloader function smoothly. Trim your brass to a uniform length, maintaining the proper SAAMI specification, as this will ensure proper headspacing; I try not to chamfer cases that headspace off the case mouth, I just like to be certain there are no burrs or rough edges on the mouth. Inspect the case rims thoroughly, discarding any with bent or damaged rims. A bent rim can result in a feeding jam, and nobody likes that. Tumble the cases well, to remove any dirt or grit before running them through the resizing dies. Clean the primer pockets and make sure your flash holes are free from any bits of media. Same with the inside of the cases. For the best accuracy, use cases of the same headstamp marking. Remember that a variation of even 0.1-grain of powder can sometimes create excessive pressure, so be certain that the powder measure is working properly and check the loads on a good scale often. Keep good records of your load data, and your handloads will serve you and your 1911 for a lifetime! Thank you, Mr. Browning.

THE GEAR

Many people who enjoy shooting their pistols frequently, be it at for gun games or just having fun at the range, will eventually consider reloading their own ammunition. The sheer volume of ammunition that can be sent downrange in a hurry requires either a large bank account and a brother-in-law who works in a sporting goods store (it's getting that difficult to obtain factory ammunition), or the ability to roll your own so that 1911 can be constantly fed. Of course, shooting your pistol often is the only way to become and remain a good shot.

Now, reloading pistol cartridges isn't a particularly difficult endeavor, but there are many variables you might do well to be aware of. You'll need a good three-die set of reloading dies, as most cartridges that work in the 1911 platform are straight walled. So, a resizing die, a flaring die and a seating die are a minimal requirement. Some companies offer a fourth die just for installing the taper crimp, but we'll get to that in just a bit.

I'd recommend buying the best dies you can afford, as they are asked to resize and reshape the brass casings possibly tens of thousands of times. I like Redding and RCBS, but I've also made huge amounts of good ammo with the more inexpensive Lee dies. Keep them properly adjusted, cleaned, and lubricated and your dies will last a lifetime.

Clean brass is a must, especially to ensure good feeding in your pistol. If you are loading new brass (that which has never been fired), you won't have to clean them before loading, but I do recommend you resize all new brass to keep things on an even playing field. If you're a range rat like I am, you'll scrounge all the once-fired brass you can get your hands on. This brass, usually picked up off the ground, can draw dirt, dust, and other foreign substances like a magnet. This brass needs to be wiped off and then cleaned in traditional methods. I've used a traditional vibratory cleaner for decades, with crushed walnut shells or

"9mm makes you weak."— Unknown

They come with either four or five stations and a rotating shell plate, so that when the press is running at full swing, up to five operations are being performed each time the handle is worked up and down. Resizing and decapping happen in the first stage, second is priming, third is case flaring, fourth a powder charge is dumped in the case, and the last station is for bullet seating and crimping. One of the issues I have with the progressive press is that during these processes you don't get an opportunity to clean the primer pocket. If you resize and remove the primer, then clean the primer pocket and continue from there, you sort of lose the speed advantage of the progressive.

If you opt not to clean the pocket, you run the long-term risk of built-up carbon and grime in the flash hole. I'm the kind of reloader who always wants to clean the primer pocket and check that the flash hole has no burrs or other problems, so that issue bugs me considerably.

Another issue I have is the priming feature of the progressive press. There are many different styles, but the same issue presents itself in every situation: there are good number of primers lined up and waiting to be mated with a cartridge case, and if one jams in sideways or is fed improperly, primer detonation is a real risk. One primer can easily set off another—or many—and, in a press that has a powder dispenser full of powder right next door, this could turn ugly in a hurry. It doesn't happen often, but it does happen.

There are a couple different ideas to circumvent these issues, but it may cut down on the production volume of the progressive press. I like to resize my

ground corn cob media, but these days I like the newer ultrasonic cleaners. They work much faster and clean both the inside and outside of the case. Twenty minutes or so in the ultrasonic, and all I need to do is toss the cases in the vibratory cleaner to give them a good shine. I always clean my brass before I resize it. This cuts down on the grit and grime that makes its way into the resizing die.

The choice of a reloading press for pistol cartridges is always a sticking point among reloaders. Many enjoy the speed and volume of production the progressive presses offer, while the opposition prefers the turret presses and single-stage operations. I'm still on the fence. Progressive presses have a lot to offer, but there are some certain drawbacks.

Redding makes the most precise dies on the market.

brass beforehand and clean the primer pockets. This ensures things are nice and neat, with no debris in the flash hole. Next, I hand prime all my cases before using the progressive. This eliminates the risk of primer detonation in the vicinity of a powder thrower. Even though it takes some extra time, I like the peace of mind knowing that I'm not sitting in front of a potential bomb.

Since I do these first steps by hand, this means I use the progressive press for case flaring, powder charging, flaring, and bullet seating. Getting the powder thrower to give the exact amount of powder you'd like takes a bit of experimentation and calibration. Some powders work better than others in the press-mounted powder measures,

spherical powders, for instance. I like Hodgdon's TiteGroup an awful lot. It is a spherical powder that meters well, gives good velocities with less powder, and has proven to be very accurate. Alliant's Unique and Bullseye are also very accurate, but being a flake-type powder, metering can be sort of tricky. The same can be said for Blue Dot and Red Dot, both of which work well in the large, high pressure cases like the 10mm Auto. I highly recommend that once you get your powder measure to throw the proper amount of powder, you check the charge every five or 10 loads on a beam scale. In many pistol cartridges, an overcharge of even 0.1-grain can result in dangerous pressures. It isn't difficult to have a powder thrower to be off by this miniscule amount, especially if the stroke of the press isn't the same each time.

Bullet seating also needs a consistent press stroke, to maintain a uniform seating depth and cartridge overall length (COL) which will, in turn, provide good feeding from the pistol's magazine. Don't be afraid to throw the micrometer on a finished case every 20 rounds or so, to make sure everything's in order. If you use your bullet seater to crimp in the same stroke, be sure that it isn't rolling the case mouth in. This could affect the cartridge headspacing and, therefore, the pistol's accuracy. I like the Lee taper crimp die, as it gives a very uniform taper crimp on the bullet portion of the case so that nothing moves out of place, yet leaves the case mouth good and square for positive headspacing.

Now, please bear in mind that the issues I have with progressive presses are not meant to scare you, just inform. Many progressive presses work without issue, for thousands of rounds. I have an RCBS Pro2000 AutoIndex that, plastic priming strip issues aside, works as advertised. It is a very consistent machine, built like a tank, and lives up to the reliability that RCBS has become famous for. My good pal Marty Groppi relies on a Dillon 550 that makes some very nice .45 ACP ammunition to feed his 1911s, and he has yet to have a single complaint. The Dillon machines are very well built and have an impeccable reputation among the progressive press lovers. Marty's 550 cranks out hundreds of rounds per week, so he's always well prepared for the weekend gun games. One feature I like about the Dillon machine is the ability to upgrade several features, such as a roller type handle to speed things up or

their audio alarm that signals low powder in the powder dispenser. They can also be dolled-up to use automatic bullet feeders and offer the option of switching out entire die plates to load for different calibers. Dillon machines also come with a lifetime warranty.

The Hornady Lock-n-Load machines also are of fine quality and have some upgrades that make a whole lot of sense. My particular favorite is the Powder Safeguard Die, a depth gauge that will detect a double charged case or a case with no powder in it at all. The first case is worse than the second, but both can be very dangerous. When the Powder Safeguard Die detects a potentially dangerous situation, it locks up the stroke of the press and delivers an audible beep that lets the operator know there's an issue. I like this kind of safety, so, when I head to the range, I know there won't be any danger other than my poor shooting!

I've devised a different manner of loading pistol ammunition quickly, but without using a progressive reloading press. It involves a good turret press and an automated powder dispenser with an electronic scale. I use a Redding T7 turret press (capable of holding up to seven reloading dies at once), and the RCBS ChargeMaster 1500 in concert to, essentially, upgrade the single-stage process to be a bit faster, yet retain the control of each step of the process. Here's what I do.

I keep the resizing, flaring, seating, and taper crimp dies in the turret, and I've even been known to keep a collet-style bullet puller on there, if I'm setting up a new bullet for proper seating depth. Since my cases are already resized (so I can clean those filthy primer pockets), and the cases are hand-primed (so I can control the primer depth by feel), I need only flare, charge the case with powder, seat a bullet, and crimp. Instead of using the mechanical, spring-loaded powder thrower, I set the RCBS ChargeMaster 1500 to dispense the exact powder charge I want, weighed out on the electronic scale. The ChargeMaster has an auto-dispense feature that weighs out another charge as soon as the pan is replaced and the scale settles to zero. In the time that it takes to dispense the powder charge, I can flare the case. The powder is then dumped into the case, using a powder funnel. Next, I switch the rotating turret head to the seating die, set the bullet on the case mouth, and seat the bullet to the proper depth. If I'm using a separate taper crimp die, I rotate the turret head again, and, in another crank of the press, that operation is done. Should I find a primer that has been seated incorrectly, or if a case mouth is kinked in the process, I have quick access to the resizing die to fix the situation. If, heaven forbid, a bullet is seated too deep, say if the seater plug should come out of adjustment, the bullet puller is also on the turret to erase my mistake, like it never happened.

Please don't get me wrong. This setup will not compete with the much higher speed of a fully functioning progressive press. What it will do is give you more control over the details of your ammunition. Seating of both primers and bullets can be held to tighter tolerances, and certainly the powder charges will be much more uniform.

For the moderate amount of pistol ammunition I unleash, this turret setup works just fine for me. When I take a 1911 to the range, it's usually for load development or accuracy assessment. I don't personally participate in the gun games, so this method produces all the ammunition I need. In addition, this method is probably the best way to avoid a double charge or no charge at all. I *need* to see that there is no powder in the case before charging and that there is a powder charge before I seat the bullet. Because I'm only charging one case at a time and then immediately seating the bullet, there is virtually no risk of a double charge.

There is absolutely nothing wrong with using a true single-stage setup for loading pistol ammunition. It takes more time and can get rather monotonous, but it works well and makes good stuff. The single-stage presses hold only one die at a time, so I usually do a minimum of 100 rounds at a time. In the same manner I load with the turret press, I keep the cases in blocks, rim up at first, initially so that I know which have been deprimed and resized, and secondly so I know which have had new primers installed. I then switch to the flaring die and set the cases rim down to be sure all the cases get flared properly. Powder is weighed and I charge one case at a time as described above. The bullet is seated when you switch the flaring die for the seater die, and then taper crimped as a final stage. The advantage of the tedious process of single-stage loading is that you truly get to inspect the cases at each point and can cull any that appear to be cracked or damaged. This is not as easy with the progressives, as you normally won't see the damaged cartridge case until the round is fully assembled.

Let's look at a couple other points to keep in mind, while reloading pistol cartridges. Keeping your dies clean, especially if you produce large quantities of ammunition, is important to maintaining dimension uniformity. Every so often, it's a good idea to disassemble the dies and thoroughly clean them. Bits of brass, burnt priming compound, and powder residue can gunk up a die. I use a good solvent like the classic Hoppe's No. 9, some cotton swabs, and lots of elbow grease to keep things clean. Sometimes (when I'm feeling lazy), I'll actually put the dies in a good ultrasonic cleaner and let them have some spa time. Be sure and give the dies a light layer of lubricant, like Rem-Oil or any other good gun oil, to prevent rust. A straightened paper clip is a good tool to clear the vent hole in the side of the dies, allowing any excess lubricant to escape. If you've purchased carbide reloading dies (which is a good idea), you won't need to lubricate the cases when resizing, but be careful not to drop these dies onto a hard surface, as there is a risk of cracking them.

I like to keep brass cases sorted out by brand, and especially in the .45 ACP, I separate out any of the newer cases that have a Small Pistol primer pocket. This is important in the progressives, as an attempt to stick a Large primer into a Small primer pocket could detonate the primer. Not good times! The brass with the small primer pocket can be reloaded using a small pistol primer, but be absolutely certain they are loaded separately and with the proper sized priming

tool, to avoid any accidents. I also like to clean and resize my brass and then keep it neatly stored until I sit down to load it. It's always nice to have a good amount of cleaned and resized brass on hand when you need to load up some ammunition for the range. I use freezer bags with a good seal or plastic coffee canisters to store my brass, and I keep them clearly labeled for future use.

Finally, because cases such as the .45 ACP, .40 S&W, and the 10mm Auto all headspace off the case mouth, I avoid putting a heavy chamfer on the case. This gives a good, square mouth for headspace in your pistol, which greatly aids in accuracy. I do like to ensure that there are no burrs on the outside edge of the case mouth that can interfere with feeding from the magazine.

If you're new to pistol reloading, start slow and become thoroughly familiar with your gear. Start your loads at the lowest charges and slowly increase the powder charge until you find the blend of accuracy and velocity that works for you. *Never* exceed the maximum charge as listed in the reloading manuals. The published data is the result of thousands of hours of testing, and to exceed the maximum is a practice that is not healthy for you or your firearm. Find the load that your pistol likes best, and you'll be able to roll out consistent ammunition for the rest of your life. Happy loading!

CHAPTER

23

MAKING THE COMPACT 1911 RIGHT

ONE THING GREAT ABOUT THE 1911, with regards to concealed carry, is that it is a flat gun. The lack of contour makes it less likely to "print," i.e., reveal its profile through clothing The problem is that it is a large gun.

Many think it's easy to simply trim the gun down to a more accommodating size. They're wrong. In fact, 1911s chambered in .45 ACP, are notorious for undependable. One very skilled gunsmith told me flat out that they just "won't run."

Bill Wilson would disagree. Unless your residence is located under a large stone, you know that his company, Wilson Combat, is producing some of the finest and most dependable custom 1911s on the planet. You also might be aware that his accessories and parts are among the best; his magazines are heralded. What you may not know is that Bill Wilson loves his compacts. In fact, he shoots them exclusively. Bill claims that the shorter sight radius is an advantage for quick target acquisition. When one with his shooting résumé speaks, one would be foolish not to listen. His accomplishments include, but are not limited to, almost 30 years of competition in multiple shooting disciplines as well as several championships. What I'm getting at, is that if Bill Wilson doesn't feel like you'ree at a disadvantage carrying a compact, why should you?

For our purposes, we'll call any 1911 with a barrel less than 4.25 inches to be a compact. Now, the reason compact 1911s have a reputation for being finicky is

A Wilson Combat CQB Compact in 9mm. It's easy to handle, reliable, and accurate.

because there isn't a whole lot of time to get everything done the gun needs to get done while the gun cycles.

Let's review what happens when you torch off a round. The hammer falls, striking firing pin which hits the primer, which sparks and ignites the powder. The bullet has no choice but to boogie off down the pipe, spinning along the path of least resistance. Meanwhile, the extractor has its little hook in the extractor groove of the case and yanks it out as the slide moves rearward. The case slams into the ejector, which flips the case out of the ejection port. As this happens, the slide is pushing the hammer back. The slide then hits the slide stop and starts its trek forward. The slide bangs into the back of the next round waiting in its place by the magazine lips. As it moves forward, the magazine spring, which has

upward tension, pushes the cartridge, nose up, as it clears the magazine lips. This nose-up position allows the slide to push the cartridge into the chamber.

Now, of course, I skipped some parts, like the fact that initially the cartridge is nose down when the slide strikes it, but you get the general idea. The bottom line is that a lot of stuff has to happen in a short amount of time. The problem with the compact 1911 is that the slide is lighter than that of of a full-length pistol. It doesn't take intimate knowledge of Newton's Second Law to understand that the lighter weight means the slide moves faster on a compact. There is simply less time to get the cartridge lifted into place—and there's the rub.

Conventional wisdom suggests that the secret to making a compact 1911 reliable is in slowing down the slide. This

A Les Baer Hemi 572. Les loves torque and recoil; the name for this pistol was inspired by the 1970 hemi 'Cuda

Les Baer Super Stinger is also a fine carry gun in .38 Super.

is accomplished both mechanically and by managing recoil.

By far, the most important consideration in this effort is the ammunition. If you want your compact 1911 to bind up, be sure to use a heavy projectile. Buffalo Bore makes a 255-grain +P it says will zap along at 1,100 fps. The recoil from such a round would slam the slide back far too fast for the gun to cycle. Please don't misunderstand what I'm saying here. Buffalo Bore makes excel-

lent ammunition, but you have to choose wisely according to the gun you're carrying. BB's 160-grain, low-recoil, standard pressure round with the Barnes bullet is an outstanding choice for a compact 1911.

The mechanical solution to the issue is pretty straightforward. First, a heavier recoil spring will slow the slide's rearward journey. This will go a long way toward solving the problem, but it's not enough; there simply isn't enough room

A Wilson Combat Super Sentinal. This compact 1911 in .38 Super is an amazing concealed carry gun.

to put adequate spring tension with just the recoil spring. Since the slide has to push the hammer back and reset it, a stouter hammer spring will, therefore, also slow down the cycle.

There are other things to consider, when creating a 1911 that is dependable as gravity, and I had the pleasure of discussing this issue with Bill Wilson. There is no debate that Bill makes some of the finest custom 1911s on the market, and his compact models are also extremely reliable. It is safe to say that no one knows more on the subject. That's because he not only builds them, he uses them almost exclusively. When Bill was shooting competitively, he used a compact 1911, and, to this day, he carries one. If they were not stone-cold reliable, you can bet that one would not be on his hip.

Bill Wilson never woke up dumb a day in his life, so it should be no surprise that he came up with an ingenious method of slowing down the slide. It is brilliant in its simplicity: a square-bottomed firing pin stop. Why does this slow the action? A normal firing pin stop is relieved, therefore, it makes contact with the hammer higher than one that is square on the bottom. Since the square-bottomed firing pin stop hits lower on the hammer, this provides less leverage as the slide pushes the hammer back against the force of the mainspring. Absolute genius.

Bill also says that the ammunition is not only important in how much recoil it produces, but also the weight of the cartridges. He says that a too-heavy "ammo stack" slows the "lift" of the spring. If it is too slow, the next cartridge won't be in position to be pushed into the chamber. He does not recommend any bullet that weighs more than 200 grains. Any more than that and the cumulative weight of a full magazine of ammunition slows down that lift.

The bottom line: A compact 1911 simply is not tuned like a full-size pistol. Extra effort needs to be taken to reduce recoil, slow the slide, and make sure the ammo stack does not weigh too much. If these things are addressed properly, your compact .45 will run just fine.

Trapper Gunworks, once famous for cutting down double action Smith and Wesson handguns, did a fine 1911 called the Scorpion.

SIGHTS FOR YOUR CARRY 1911

THERE ARE LIES, DAMNED LIES, and statistics. The numbers will tell you that most self-defense shootings happen really fast, really close, and with only a few shots fired. In fact, the old timers would speak of the "Rule of Three": Three shots, inside of three yards, in a maximum of three seconds. Well, heck, why do we have sights at all?

It turns out we don't often use our sights under stress. After all, if there's a bad guy, a guy so bad that we are shooting, we are probably focused on him, not our gun. This is why the most skilled shooter is prone to making some horrible shots when the chips are down. What's the solution?

In such a defense situation, the sights need to be quickly acquired and, since bad things can happen any time of the day, they also need to work in low light conditions. One solution gun designers came up with is the three-dot system. The theory is that that you line up the dots, simple and easy, and your weapon is properly aligned with the target. The problem with this is that, under stress, you are probably going to be focused on the bad guy not lining up dots. Even in the best of defensive situations, you want a fast "flash sight picture." The idea is that the front sight needs to be on target for just a moment, for acceptable target acquisition before you squeeze the trigger. With this in mind, you want less visual "noise" at the rear. In my opinion, having twice as many "dots" in the back is the wrong way to go.

The problem is that we can't focus on the rear sight, the front sight, and the target at the same time. The eyes just don't work that way. Conventional wisdom says you should always focus on the front sight and let everything else be fuzzy. While this is a nice theory, in reality, our eyes will naturally go to the threat, the target. This is not to say that teaching looking at the front sight is bad, quite the contrary, in fact. By keeping the front sight as a priority in the shooter's mind, when under stress, it is possible they will see it at all, even subconsciously. As for the rear sight, the best kind for a defensive carry gun is to have on that doesn't attract the eye, so nothing busy.

Since the front sight's the more important of the two (again, I'm talking about for defensive carry, here), how do you make it visible? One is with fiber optics. Sure, they can look a little cheesy, but they often work well, even in low light conditions. Let us remember, a defensive weapon is a tool, not a fashion accessory. Function should always win over style, when lives are on the line.

Some fiber fiber optic sights do surprisingly well in no-light conditions, though they have to have at least some sort of light source to make them glow. A weapon light can illuminate them, as can a tactical light. Conventional wisdom suggests that green is more easily seen in low-light conditions. I confess that my aging eyes have issues in the

dark, so the brighter the better. Because of this, I actually prefer red. Is it because my Hayes Custom has a red fiber optic front sight and I am used to it, or is the red truly brighter? I know not, but I do not have any green replacement tubes for my fiber optic sights.

Making the front sight glow-in-the-dark with tritium inserts is another good idea. The eye is drawn to light, so your focus will be at the front of your muzzle. This is a help to me in the middle of the night, so that I can more easily locate my gun on the nightstand. If I pick it up, the glowing front sight helps me ascertain that I have a proper grip.

As to the rear sight, its job is to help you line up the front sight with the target, with minimal disruption to the sight picture. Wayne Novak recognized this when he invented his rear sight, a simple, wedge-shaped blade with a wide rear notch. Tritium rear sights are *not* a good idea for a self-defense or carry gun. There is twice as much "light" at the rear, and the chances of putting them in the wrong order is very real, especially under pressure.

There's a sighting system for 1911s (and other guns) that's pretty interesting. It is the XS Big Dot. As I mentioned, when the target is a threat, we tend to focus on it. What a lot of smart folks learned is that a highly visible front sight was key to successful hits on such threats. Who might those smart people be? Jeff

A Springfield Operator with adjustable XS Big Dot sights and a weapon light. It's an ideal combination for home-defense.

The large front sight is amazingly easy to pick up under stress, and the shallow "V" gets out of the way.

Cooper, W.E. Fairbain, Rex Applegate, Bill Jordan, Massad Ayoob, Jim Cirillo, Clint Smith, Charles Askins, and a host of others. A big, easy to pick up front sight is key to seeing your front sight under stress.

Of course, in a time when you need to defend yourself, that front sight isn't going to be in focus—your eyes will be focused on the bad guy—and that's why it has to be big. But what about the rear sight? The function of the rear sight is to give the shooter something with which to frame and center the front sight, thus, a wide, shallow, unadorned "V" is all that's needed.

This is not a new concept. Rifles made to hunt dangerous African game have express sights, which are much like the XS system, with a wide, shallow "V" rear sight and a large, high-visibility front sight.

It is not a new concept for self-defense

weapons, either. William E. Fairbain and his colleague Eric A Sykes developed a nearly identical system when they were on the front lines in Shanghai, in the 1930s; it is hard to imagine the violence they faced there on a regular basis. Armed encounters were a daily occurrence. Fairbain and Sykes co-authored a book, published in 1942, entitled Shooting to Live, in which they describe their solution to pistol sights:

[F]or long shots, as we have been describing, sights offer a distinct advantage. We have little faith, however, in those furnished. Good as some are for use against a white target and a black bull's eye, there are very few that can be picked up against a dark background, and this difficulty is increased to the point of being insuperable when the light is bad. To overcome this, the authors' personal pistols are fitted with foresights of sil-

ver, of exactly the shape of the ordinary shot-gun bead and the same size. If kept bright, these sights collect any light there is from any angle and can be seen instantly in all circumstances except pitch-darkness. ... Though not claimed as suitable for target work, these sights answer their primary purpose admirably, where speed is the primary consideration.

Sounds a lot like an XS Big Dot front sight, but again, what about the rear? The two worte, that "The best rear sight for use in conjunction with the silver bead is the a wide and shallow "V."

In his book *Handgun Training For Personal Protection* (available at www.gundigeststore.com), Richard Mann referred to the fact that Jeff Cooper used XS Big Dot sights on his personal gun. While I never had the pleasure to meet Col. Cooper, from everything I've read about and by him, he was a serious sort. He surely would not put sights on his gun because of a fad or for style points.

This all sounds good and well in theory, but what about in practice? I put a set of XS Big Dot sights on a Kimber Ultra+ CDP II. For those unfamil-

iar with the gun, it is an alloy framed .45 with a full-size grip but a three-inch barrel. It is not the easiest gun to shoot, due to its barrel length and lack of weight, but the full-size grip helps a lot.

The XS Big Dot came with everything you need to install it, save a brass or nylon gunsmith hammer. Find one of those hammers and then simply use the supplied nylon drift punch and tap the old sight out and the new one in. A drop of thread locker like Locktite is also a good idea.

I used a micrometer to get my Big Dot in the center and went to the range. Wow. These things just *work*. My splits went down significantly and target transitions were very smooth. It is truly amazing how fast you can pick up the front sight and get the gun on target. The sight picture is instantaneous. I am sold on it.

That is not to say that this sight is the only way to go. There are a lot of smart guys out there with Novak or Novak-style sights. I find the rear groove to be too narrow for my aging eyes, but your mileage may vary. Bill Wilson favors a fiber optic front sight and a wide opening on the flat black rear sight. They're sights—not ridiculously expensive (for the most part), so go through the choices until you find what works for you and your 1911. There might be one day when you're really going to appreciate the time you put into finding this small but important piece of gear.

The Springfield Micro is an outstanding carry choice.

CHAPTER 25

TACTICAL LIGHTS: PROS AND CONS

WHILE BAD THINGS DON'T HAPPEN EXCLUSIVELY at night, it sure seems like they do. When something goes bump in the night, in addition to your 1911, you need a good light.

There are many positive aspects to a weapon-mounted light. For one, it's automatically with the gun, so, you know right where it is. Your spouse didn't it borrow it to look for the cat last night and forgot to return it, and you didn't take it out of the kitchen junk drawer and leave it in your pickup's glove compartment. Another great aspect of a weapon-mounted light is that, when you use it, it is pointed where you need it. Since most shootings occur in low-light conditions, this can be a very, very good thing. On the other hand, one tends to point the business end of the gun at things they want to illuminate, even though they don't want to shoot it. This, of course, breaks one of the primary rules of gun safety.

Like anything else, you have to consider the downside with the up. For instance, in addition to illuminating things you don't necessarily want to shoot, weapon lights, while not heavy compared to the old 8-cell Brinkman that cops used to carry, do add weight to your firearm. Enough weight to matter? Possibly. Another downside? While you have the benefit of always having illumination where you need, a powerful advantage in a defensive situation, on the other hand, the light flags your position. Some prefer a handheld light held at arm extension away from their body, so as to not draw fire to the light. The downside to that is that you may end up shooting

YAMIL SUED PHOTO

one-handed.

Another problem with pistol-mounted lights occurs when holstering the weapon. Safariland and other companies make some holsters specifically for guns with lights. That's good, but they can be cumbersome and are usually not as fast to draw from as a regular duty-type holster, let alone a slick Kydex rig. If yours is a home-defense weapon, of course, you might not need a holster.

One of the best reasons to use a pistol-mounted light is that you can use both hands to grip the gun. If you are using a handheld, by definition you have to use a hand on the light. Unless you resemble Ganesh, you will then only have one remaining hand with which to grip the gun. For those of you who think you

are just as good with one hand as you are with two, I challenge you to shoot a match, be it IDPA, USPSA, or Steel Challenge, with only one hand. The results can be quite sobering. Don't ask me how I know.

As to the aspect of using your weapon to illuminate the items that should not have a gun pointed at them, this is a real concern, but it's one that can be overcome with training. One example is holding the gun at low ready, where the light can illuminate enough of what you need to see without having the gun pointed at something it should be. Another factor is that just because you have a pistol-mounted light doesn't mean you can't carry another light. I am pretty sure that there is no rule, law, or regulation

that says you are limited to one. Darn, I hope I didn't give them any ideas.

So, let's say you've decided to use a pistol-mounted light. Which one do you choose? There are a lot of choices for the 1911, and, when I say a lot, I mean a *lot*. Literally hundreds of companies are producing tactical pistol-mounted lights. When going through the plethora of choices there are several things to consider.

The first is the output of the light. Generally speaking, more is better. That said, too much of a good thing becomes a bad thing. In a home-defense situation, your surroundings are, by nature, very tight. Mirrors, windows, and even walls can reflect your light into your eyes. This has the inverse effect of what you should

be looking for, which is to blind the bad guy and make him an easier target for you.

Another consideration is that the mega-bright lights are great, but they use a lot of power. This means that you are out of juice faster. Unlike the governmental powers, you probably have to buy your own batteries and probably won't throw them away until they are spent. Governments, since they are using our money, will put fresh cells into their lights before an operation or even a shift. These bing the facts of life, the home-defender may be better served by using a light that is less bright and, therefore, less likely to fade when needed. Also, more power requires more batteries, which means more bulk and weight. Neither one is a

Sig Sauer has several models that come with weapon lights and lasers.

Nighthawk GRP with Surefire X300.

good thing when attached to your 1911.

You next need to consider the light's actual beam. A beam of light is a three-dimensional shape, and there are three styles available in today's tactical lights: spot beam, flood beam, and the combination beam.

A spot beam is just like it sounds. A narrow, tightly focused cone that is best for maximizing the distance at which the beam is effective. This is a good thing when the distances are greater, meaning outdoors or in a large room. Of course, this means it is also not the best idea for tighter spaces. The eyes are drawn to light and movement so, naturally, the narrow beam is where they focus. This leads to tunnel vision.

A flood beam is a wide-angle beam that bathes an area in light. The great

thing about a flood beam is that it is a more natural light and less likely to have hot spots and reflection issues. This makes you less prone to tunnel vision, as your peripheral vision is more engaged. The downside to this beam style is that the range of the light is limited.

Many consider the combination beam to be the best of both worlds, while others consider it neither fish nor fowl. In such a light, the narrow spot beam is surrounded by a broader flood beam. While this sounds good on paper, in reality, the lights usually have hot spots and a dark area where the reflector angles change. In close quarters, the spot part of the beam can still cause reflection, which can affect your vision. That said, the possibility of acquiring tunnel vision is considerably less, as the flood

The weight of the light helps control muzzle flip.

ous to do when you should be looking at the threat—is a good thing. The problem is that a large, easy to operate switch is also easy to operate inadvertently if you bump into something.

As to mounting your light, if your gun has a rail, you are golden. Clamp that baby on and use some blue Locktite or other thread locker. If not, there are mounts that attach to the trigger guard. While I am not a fan, some have reported good results.

No matter which light you choose, handheld or pistol-mounted, it is imperative for you to train with it in low light conditions. The first step is to, with an unloaded gun in your empty house, move around and see what everything looks like. Trust me, it will not look the same as it does when the lights are on. The areas that you can see versus the ones bathed in light are obvious, and the revelation can sometimes be startling. At the same time, look at how vulnerable *you* are. While you are looking down the hall in one direction, you make a nice target down the other. Note the reflections, hot spots and other issues. Some, you will be able to handle, like moving a mirror to another location. Others you will just have to deal with. It is better to know the challenges ahead of time.

The next thing to do is to actually shoot at night. Of course, most ranges do not allow anyone to shoot in low or no light conditions, but some allow night matches. In central Texas, Copperas Cove Pistol Club, for instance, will put on some matches at night—trust me, it can be illuminating, pun intended. You quickly learn just how bad a shot you are. You learn the inadequacies of your equipment. You learn just how slow you are. It is humbling, to say in the least.

segment of the beam is illuminating the periphery.

Another consideration in your light choice, which is, in my mind, paramount, is the light's switch. Many favor a pressure switch that turns the light on when the hand grips the gun. The problem with these designs is that a proper grip on the gun also means the light is on. This is not necessarily something you want. On the other hand, you don't have to think about it in a high stress situation. A nice, ergonomic switch that does not require you to look at it—something difficult to do in the dark and danger-

CHAPTER 26

LASER SIGHTS ON THE CUSTOM 1911

ASERS FOR HANDGUNS HAVE come a long way over the years, but when it comes to putting one on your gun for home-defense, the crowd is still divided.

There are some good reasons *not* to go to the light. They can break, run out of battery power, and otherwise be undependable. They are hard to see in bright light. In addition, they take the focus away from the front sight, the epicenter of all pistol shooting. Finally, if more than one gun in an area has a laser, it is easy to get confused.

On the other hand, they are great tools in addition to the sights. Lots of instructors are quickly coming to understand that they are outstanding training devices. Why? They do not require a sight picture to know that you are on target.

Those are just a couple of the pros and cons. Let's take a deeper look at the issues, starting with the negatives.

Dependability is one of the main reasons to shun the laser. It is a battery operated light, and, just like a flashlight is nothing more than an aluminum tube in which one stores dead batteries, the laser sight can be nothing but an ugly grip when there's no power source.

Another potential problem is that you might not be the only laser in the situation. If you are looking for a red dot and there is more than one, confusion is sure to follow.

Some suggest that the laser can reveal your location. For the civilian, I don't see

Crimson Trace is a leader in the field of weapon lasers.

how this is much of a problem, but it is a possibility. If you are in the middle of a home invasion and are pointing the gun down the hallway, waiting for the intruder, he might recognize the fact that you have a gun. This is likely to give him pause, but it is also possible that revealing your location can be used against you.

On the flip side, no matter how much we expound, preach, and proselytize about focusing on the front sight, when the action starts, we are going to look at the threat. The laser allows one to focus on the threat, which would occur naturally anyway. From a purely practical standpoint, they add insignificant weight to a 1911 (lights can definitely make them front-heavy), and most laser designs don't require a special holster.

Another huge advantage is knowing that you are on target when you can't see your sights. If you are close to the threat or, as Jeff Cooper would say, "the goblin," it is unwise to put the gun within their reach. Many a person has been disarmed

YAMIL SUED PHOTO

the police arrive? Even in an urban area, police response time is measured in minutes. I have read that the average police response time in the U.S. is around 10 minutes but I also read that in one particular crime-ridden city, they police department was bragging about getting their response time down—down!—to 24 minutes. Even if you're a gym rat, you can't keep a gun at eye level for half an hour. I know I wouldn't want to do so for the average response time. Even if you could, what's happening to your motor skills during that time? Trust me, they are diminishing. The laser, then, allows you to relax, hold the gun close to the body, elbows down, even shift from hand to hand while assuring that the muzzle is pointed at the threat.

While I am a fan of the laser as a sighting tool, I am equally as big of a fan of it as a training tool. A laser shows a new shooter where their muzzle is, when they're handling a gun. It is a lot less clumsy than my old method of using a rubber band to attach a penlight to the pistol, in an awkward attempt to teach a student safe gun handling. Beyond first safety lessons, though, the laser is truly an outstanding training tool for any shooter. Hold a sight picture and squeeze the trigger. If you have not done so before, you will be surprised at how much the beam on that paper target moves. Trigger discipline, or the lack thereof, is instantly revealed.

Want to practice target transitions? Lasers are an tool for that. Do it low on the wall (with an empty gun), and it also gives the cat some exercise. The bottom line is that the laser reveals what is really happening with the muzzle of the gun, not just what you think is happening.

by holding their pistol out. Professionals are taught a quick, efficient, and nearly foolproof method of extracting a pistol from a combatant; it is silly to suggest that only the good guys know how to do this. So, the laser allows you to keep the handgun close to your body and still know that it is on target. This is not only important for close-quarters situations, but also if you have to hold your gun on a target for a long period of time. Why would this happen? How about if you have to keep near your assailant until

CHAPTER
27

DRY-FIRING THE CUSTOM 1911: YES YOU CAN!

DRY-FIRING IS AN EXTREMELY EFFECTIVE way to practice shooting. One not only strengthens the hand and fingers, but it helps with muscle memory, trigger control, and maintaining a good sight picture. Sure, some people will tell you that dry-firing will damage your firing pin. They say that the pin, since it doesn't have anything to slam into, will be damaged. Really? Know this about your 1911: If your firing pin has a deformity that will cause it to fail dry-firing, it will fail while live-firing, too. In that respect, dry-firing is a test to see if your firing pin sucks. This kind of testing might save your life, if you need the gun in a defensive situation. So ignore the naysayers who are just looking for something to whine about. Dry-fire away.

I have read that many firearms instructors recommend a 70/30 split between dry-fire and live-fire drills. That's right, 70 percent dry-fire, 30 percent live-fire, the mindset being that you need to get your actions and technique down before you start wasting ammo. I have to agree, especially with the cost of ammunition these days. Add the fact that, after 5,000 repetitions, an act becomes hardwired into your brain. You might as well do it right.

With this in mind, you have to do it right—no, you have to do it *perfectly*—every time. This means starting your dry-fire practice slowly—*very* slowly. Being perfect is more important that doing so quickly. Speed will come in time.

Of course, before you do any dry-firing, make sure the gun is unloaded and use a

Laser Ammo is a great training tool, especially in a Wilson CQB compact

chamber flag. I also suggest you remove all live ammunition from the area. Gear up and stand up. While not necessary, some small, physical targets are fun, especially if you are training for the gun games. Little IDPA or IPSC targets are cool.

Set a goal for your training. Let us say that you want to work on your first shot, or maybe it's your target transitions.

Work on one element of the thing you want to perfect, and one element only before moving on to the next and, eventually, putting all the elements together. I like to start from the beginning, the draw. Practice, very slowly, getting the proper grip on the gun while it's in the holster, retrieving the gun from the holster, and then bringing it to target. Do this at least 20 times. Concentrate, Grasshopper. Forget speed. It is all about muscle memory. The speed will come.

If you are training with the 1911, you not only need a good grip on the gun, you need to get a good thumb position on the safety. Remember, you have to ride the safety. Not only can you only press it down if your thumb is on top of it, if you allow your thumb to go any other place, it will affect your grip and, possibly, during recoil, engage it enough to lock up your gun. The only proper place for your strong thumb is on top of the safety, period.

Many will tell you that, if they ride the safety, they can't depress the grip safety. This is usually true only if the safety is oversized. That said, many people will pin the grip safety, thus holding it down automatically and, effectively, rendering it's original intention for being useless. This is *not* legal in the shooting sports, where no safety device may be disengaged. In the real world, the grip safety is not a necessary device. Remember, the 1911 was not originally designed with a grip safety. The federal government, an entity renowned for its stupidity and inefficiency, is the entity that required the grip safety. When John Moses was designing his next incarnation on the 1911 design, unencumbered by government intervention, there was no grip safety. Of course, I am speaking of the Browning Hi-Power.

When dry-firing, you need to focus on the front sight. Your eyes can't focus on the rear sight, front sight, and target, nothing new here. If you can see the front sight and keep the target fuzzy, out of focus, you can know where your gun is pointed.

Remember to squeeze, not yank the trigger. Do you pull the gun off target as the trigger is pulled? There's a great way to figure this out. A company named Sure Strike makes a training device called the Laser Training Cartridge. It is a cartridge that you put into your chamber and, when the hammer strikes it, a laser beam is illuminated, showing you where the round would have hit. It is a very high-quality product, and it's totally secure, in that not only can a live round not be chambered with the Laser Ammo cartridge in the chamber, there is also a safety pipe that sticks out the end of the barrel, alerting you that the gun is inert. The cool thing about it is that it is truly activated by the firing pin. Except for the boom and the recoil, it is exactly like live fire. This is outstanding for seeing how your gun is moving, which it shouldn't, when you pull the trigger. We all sometimes have a tendency to slap a trigger, and this product lets us know what the penalty is for doing so (usually a laser "hit" that's to the right). The Sure Strike Laser Training Cartridge comes with an electronic target, too. It reacts to the laser and keeps your score. It can also be programmed to beep, to prompt your draw. If there's any drawback to using one with a single-action 1911, it is that, of course, the action doesn't cycle, so you'll have to cock the hammer back every time you want to pull the trigger.

THE 1911 EXTRACTOR: IT'S NO SMALL THING

EVERYONE KNOWS THAT ONE OF THE KEYS to making your 1911 run, whether that gun is custom or stock, is to tune its extractor. Oh, sure, the magazine may be the most important factor in reliability, but the extractor is undoubtedly second.

If you look at your 1911's extractor, at first glance, it seems to be nothing more than a simple little hook. Well, it is a little hook, but it's not simple.

Now, one might think that a little hook that yanks the spent shell casing out of the chamber would be pretty much foolproof. This is not the case. If the tension is too tight, it can't slip past the case head if it doesn't get there in time. If it is too loose, it won't grab the spent shell at all. And, if it twists, it won't consistently get a good purchase on the case and, thus, will not extract dependably.

The first thing you need to understand is that the hook is not designed to slip over the case head. It is supposed to slide into the grove as the slide moves forward. The bevel on the end is in case the timing is imperfect and still let extractor can slip over the edge. With this in mind, proper tension is a must. In a perfect world; the extractor groove will be filled with the case head. Upon firing, the slide will travel back, carrying the extractor with it to yank out the spent brass then slam it into the ejector to cause that beautiful arc of brass over your right shoulder.

How do you tell if your extractor tension is tuned right? Let's take a look.

After checking your gun, field strip it. Take a loaded cartridge and slip it under the extractor hook. Do not use an empty cartridge; the weight of a loaded cartridge is required for this (and, as is the case with any live ammo, make sure you're in a safe environment to do so). Make sure the round is positioned as if the gun were fully assembled. This is done by lining up the centerline of the cartridge with the center of the extractor. Now, if you shake it (a gentle shake), does the round fall out? If it did, it's time to adjust your extractor.

There are two schools of thought on the method for adjusting the tension of your extractor. The most common is that you slide the first half-inch or so into the extractor channel and give it a little push to the side, bending it slightly. This bends it adjacent to the widest point. The other school of thought suggests that tapping it with a hammer, in the middle, is the best. In fact, there's a tool available from Brownells that does this very thing. Personally, I've fond that laying it across the open jaws of a vice and using a gunsmithing hammer seems to work fine.

Which method is better? I opine that getting the bend in the middle is the best outcome. This puts the front-most hook end of the extractor at a better angle than if the bend is farther back. Is it enough to make a difference? Probably not. Have I used the extractor channel to adjust my extractor in the field? You bet.

There is another factor to consider when adjusting your extractor, and that is the position. If you look at the groove in which the case head fits, the back of that is called the "locator pad." You want that pad contacting the case with about a pound of pressure. The best way to check this is to slide an empty case into under the extractor, making sure the hook grabs it at the centerline. The empty case should be held in place firmly, able to take a light shake without falling out. If you pull the case down, there should be a miniscule amount of movement. The experts say .075- to .1000-inch, but I have never measured. The real test is when you put a loaded cartridge under the extractor. A light shake should have it falling out.

CHAPTER 29

COMMON ISSUES THAT SIDELINE YOUR CUSTOM 1911

YOU HAVE SPENT A TON OF MONEY on a custom 1911. You have showed your buddies, and they have drooled on it. Yes, it is a beautiful gun, and it was made just for you. The joy and pride that you feel is amazing—until you have a problem, because then you feel ripped off, betrayed, and embarrassed. We have all been there. Let's look at the most common issues and their solutions.

Probably, behind magazines, the No. 1 problem a 1911 shooter will come across is with ammunition. Light primer strikes, failure to chamber, or failure to feed can be the result of your ammunition. The most common of these ills is a light primer strike, something usually caused by an improperly seated primer. Before a match, I take my ammunition and rub a thumb across the case head. You should not feel the primer stick above at all. In a perfect world, it should be perfectly flat. Actually, the reloading manuals say that it should be recessed into the primer pocket by .003-inch. My thumb isn't that sensitive, and, no, I do not measure. If you want to be super precise, lay a straight edge across the case head. The side of a stainless steel pocket ruler is outstanding for this. The primer should not touch the straight edge. Another way to check is to stand up the round. If it rocks back and forth, the primer hasn't been seated deeply enough. Does that mean it should not be used? Of course not. Just use it for plinking ammo instead of for a huge match (or your home-defense load).

As for a handloader solving the issue of their primers not being seated deeply

keeping extra parts is required when you run your gun hard.

enough, that's a relatively easy fix. Either adjust your press or, if you are using a hand priming tool, bear down a little harder. It is usually just a matter of seating pressure.

What if it looks like you're getting light primer strikes, but you are sure the primer is seated properly. If this is your case, you probably have "primer flow."

Primer flow is caused by too much cartridge pressure, and it usually occurs when you are shooting hot loads. What happens is that the primer tries to push into the firing pin hole. The primer and the firing pin, fighting to occupy the same space, leave some detritus on the edge of the firing pin hole. This can slow the movement of the firing pin and stop it from giving your primer a good enough whack to set it off. Usually it takes several rounds having their primer

material being sheared off in the firing pin hole before they cause an issue, but not always. One very bad flowing primer can stop your 1911 in its tracks.

Fixing primer flow is easy. Simply adjust your load. Switch powders, switch primers, switch recipes, switch factory loads. Make some test loads, grab your chronograph and head to the range. Check your firing pin hole after every shot. With my failing eyes, I bring a magnifying glass so that I can look for the slightest amount of primer residue in the firing pin hole. Also, look that the primer itself. You don't what to see too much of a bulge around the firing pin indention.

If you do have primer flow, you need to clean up the mess it's left. A .22 LR bore brush works great, as does a pipe cleaner. Wearing eye protection, a spray of solvent and some compressed air does wonders. The primer material is usually not stuck on really tight; sometimes even a Q-tip will work to dislodge it.

If your gun is failing to chamber, you might have a little more of a mystery on your hands. While my experience suggests that it is your ammunition, it could be as simple as gunk in the chamber. That's easy to deal with. Remove the gunk and keep shooting. If there is nothing obvious restricting the cartridge from sliding freely into the chamber, take a close look at the round in question. Does it chamber check? If not, it could be that the bullet is not seated deeply enough and, therefore, the overall length is out of spec. Consult your reloading manual, adjust your press, and your problem is solved.

Another possibility is that your brass hasn't been properly sized. Shame on you, but it's still an easy fix. Get the resizing die set properly, double-checking with your reloading manual, and start yanking that lever. Problem solved.

A bad crimp on the bullet can cause problems. Your crimp should be smooth and angled in just a bit. A bullet seated too low in the case can cause a bulge, too. Get back to the reloading bench and get your dies set right. A good caliper and a reloading book are necessary.

Another possibility is that the extractor is too tight. This is easily checked. Field strip your gun and place an empty case under the extractor, with the centerlines of the slide and the case aligned. The case should stay in place if you give it a gentle shake. I mean a gentle shake. On the other hand, a loaded cartridge should *not* stay if you conduct the same test. A pound to a pound and a half of pressure are what you're looking for.

There is one more thing to look for and that's the extractor hook's relation to the breech face. Grab your caliper and check and see if it is too tight. You are looking for between .006- and .075-inch, depending on whom you ask. In my experience, aiming for the middle is a good strategy.

Failure to feed is almost always the fault of the magazine, but, if you have one, take a look at the ammunition. Check for the overall length of your cartridges. If your ammo is in spec, the bane of your 1911 is its magazine.

REQUIRED MAINTENANCE

GOOD MAINTENANCE IS KEY to keeping your custom 1911 running well. In addition, it is also important to keep it from wearing; after all, grimy lube is nothing but a lapping compound. But how much maintenance is enough?

Our daddies and granddaddies taught us that every time we shoot our gun we should clean it. They were not wrong. Back in the day, the primers were corrosive. Letting a gun sit all cruddy could damage it, leaving pits in the chamber and the bore. But those days are, thankfully, gone, as modern primers are noncorrosive. That said, some powders are dirty and leave a lot of residue. In addition to being abrasive, they can muck up the works.

So how often is enough? I have to tell you, I don't clean my 1911s very often. Every third to fifth match. However, I lube it every time I finish shooting it. Even that raises a question. Ed Brown says, if you're not getting oil on your forearm as you shoot, your gun needs oil. Bill Wilson says too much oil attracts dirt and that it only needs it where it needs it. Who's right? Sounding like a politician I will say, it depends. Before we get into that, let's break down that gun.

FIELD STRIPPING

First, before you do anything, put on some eye protection. Yes, springs can launch parts, which can do damage to your eyes. In addition, you will be using solvents, and eyes are not partial to those either. Put on some shooting glasses.

Second, check the gun to make sure it's empty. Twice. Remove all live ammo from the area. Check the gun again. I know, I know. You know all these rules, but I would be remiss were I not to remind you. Diligence saves lives.

Using a bushing wrench, depress the recoil spring plug and rotate the bushing clockwise about 90 degrees, as you look at the muzzle. Holding onto the recoil spring plug, let it slowly out. This is a good place to launch it, as the spring tension is waiting to bounce it off of your forehead. Let the spring push the bushing out, under control, and remove it. Now, make sure the safety is disengaged and push the slide back until the little round cutout is aligned with the back of the slide stop on the left side of the slide. From the right side of the slide, push the slide stop from right to left, out of the gun. Yes, it takes a little effort.

At this point I like to turn the gun upside down, sights on the bench, and slide the frame off of the back of the slide. This is my method, because it stops parts from falling out and bouncing under the bench where it takes me 10 minutes of cursing to find them. Next, delicately remove the guide rod and recoil spring, with special attention to keeping the spring from getting tangled. Grab your bushing wrench and rotate it in the other direction, counter clockwise, and, when the tabs on the bushing line up, remove it. If it is particularly tight, just push the barrel forward. If properly aligned, it will come right out. Be sure to push the barrel link forward as you do this.

Your gun is now field stripped. Every 600 to 1,000 rounds, I break down my competition gun, a Hayes Custom, to this point and give her a good, basic cleaning.

Most probably the feed-ramp and the rails will be caked with burnt gunpowder and lubricant. Use some Hoppe's No. 9 and soak the gunk, then set aside. The barrel, bushing, recoil spring, and recoil spring plunger, I spray down with brake cleaner.

There is another method that none other than Bill Wilson recommends in his book *The Combat Auto.* He dips these parts, including the whole slide, into a commercial paint preparation solvent made by DuPont called Prep Sol. It is available at some auto parts stores and automotive paint supply fronts. It is designed to remove all grease from the surface of a car prior to painting. I have never used it, but Bill says it is a great product.

Bill recommends putting the Prep Sol into a military ammo can and soaking the parts. Of course, this is pretty tough stuff, so use in a well-ventilated area (outside) and wear rubber gloves. In five minutes or less, your gun parts are clean.

Another friend of mine has an automotive parts washer. It is basically a sink or tub-like apparatus with a nozzle that recirculates the solvent. The nozzle is flexible, so that you can aim it where dirtiest parts are. The advantage is that the movement of the solvent also helps to flush away the crud.

Some of the gunk and grime will not come off readily. I use a small brass brush, about the size of a toothbrush, to scrape away the sludge. An old one works well.

While a step farther than field stripping, I will take the ejector out and make sure it is clean, too. It is simple to remove and much more accessible to clean

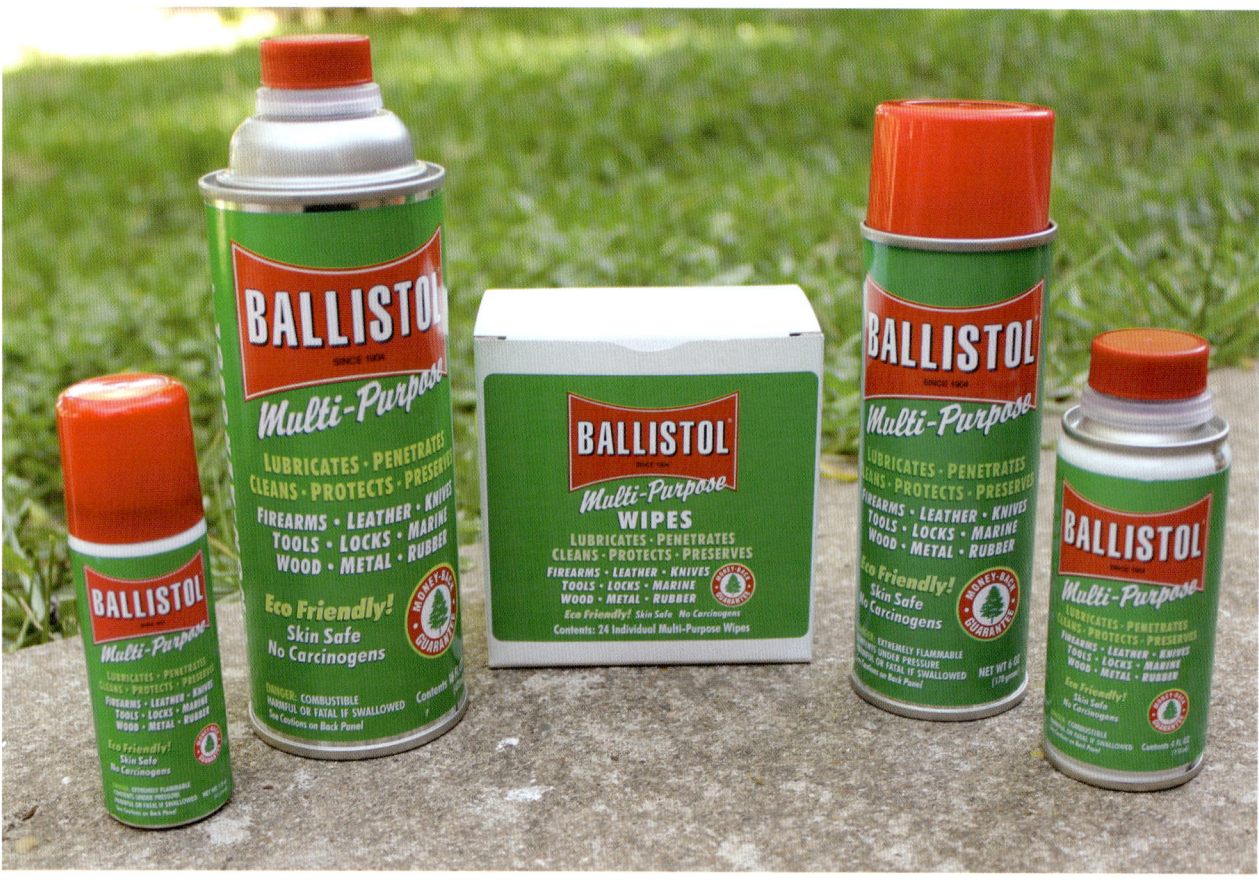

Good quality lubricants are essential

when not installed. This is accomplished very easily. Pick up the slide and, using a punch, push in the firing pin. The firing pin stop then slides off, but, remember, it's spring-loaded. I aim it towards my chest in case I mess up and launch it. As the firing pin stop slides clear of the firing pin, be ready with your thumb to catch it. If not, it will go far. Don't ask me how I know.

The firing pin channel usually isn't too dirty. A spray of your favorite solvent will usually take care of it. Same thing for the extractor channel. The frame rails, on the other hand, will need some work. Your spray solvent and a brush will usually do a good job, but a bamboo skewer will help plow it out.

Since we are already past the tradi-

tional field strip, let's take it down all the way. Go ahead and remove the grips. While the two screws on either side are no problem to figure out, sometimes they have an extremely tight fit in the frame insert. If this is the case, usually reaching up into the magazine well and pushing outward will make them pop off.

An important note is required here: While the slide is off, do *not* pull the trigger! The hammer should not be allowed to slam into the frame.

With the hammer back, put the safety to the point where it is fully depressing the spring, the place where it doesn't want to be. Grabbing the tab of the safety, wiggle back and forth, trying to lift the pin out. It helps to push on it from the other side. This is the pin on which the grip safety hinges, so you should be able to find it. As it comes out, the spring and plungers, which keep the safety either up or down, might pop out. If not, use a pin to gently push it to the rear and it will fall right out. (Note that the small plunger is towards the front of the gun. This will help when reassembling.) Cautiously, without dropping it, lower the hammer lightly. This takes the pressure off of the mainspring, which is what we are going to remove next. Take a pin and a very small hammer and drift the pin found at the bottom of the mainspring housing from left to right. Tap gingerly; do *not* hammer this. Softly tap the pin. While it may be recalcitrant at first, it will soon move freely. More little taps are better than one big one. Make sure that there is room for the pin to exit the other side.

As you slide the mainspring out of the bottom of the frame, the grip safety will fall, unceremoniously, onto the bench. There is a flat spring, the sear spring, that will pull out easily. You will note that the spring has three tines. This is because it is actually the spring for the sear, the disconnector, and the grip safety. This is a long-winded description, so most everyone calls it the sear spring. It is important to note the function of each one, because you may have to bend it to adjust.

Next, you need to remove the hammer pin and the sear pin. Just punch them out, gently. The parts will freely drop out.

All you have left at this point is to remove is the trigger. Push in the magazine release just a little bit and turn the screw on the right side of the trigger guard. It is important to note that it is *not* a screw, so don't try to remove it. Just rotate it and wiggle the magazine release. It takes a bit to get it into just the right place, but, when it aligns properly, it drops out as a single unit. With that, the trigger should drop free, and you now have a disassembled 1911. Of course full-length guide rods and ambidextrous safeties add a couple other steps, but this is the basic disassembly. Pretty cool, eh?

Now, using brake cleaner, Prep Sol, Break Free CLP, Hoppes, whatever your favorite cleaner is, get everything sparkling clean. After everything's clean and dry, while all of the parts do not need lubrication, they do require rust protection. So, at this time I will spray them down with lubricant and wipe down, leaving a thin, protective coat of oil.

REASSEMBLY

In the greater scheme of things, doing what you did in reverse order is what you are supposed to do, but it isn't quite that simple.

Sliding the trigger back in and putting the magazine release in are pretty straightforward operations. Yeah, a little back and forth manipulation to get it together is required as you put the magazine release back in, but it's still easy.

The hardest part is to get the sear pin back in. I use tweezers. It helps hold the sear and the disconnector together in that small place in the frame. Still, it is a tricky operation and the hardest part of putting your custom 1911 back together. What I like to do is to get the pin started in the sear so that it holds it in place, and then manipulate the disconnector into position. I actually use the firing pin from the right side to line up the holes. Then I insert the sear pin from the left side, following the firing pin through the holes.

The hammer is pretty straightforward. Positioning the hammer down, just nimbly tap it in. Do *not* cock the hammer, as it will cause problems when you go to put the mainspring housing back together. If you do pull the hammer back, just pull the trigger and push it forward. No sweat.

Rotating the hammer strut out of the way, set the sear spring. The bottom has a ninety-degree bend, which fits into a slot, so it can only go in one way.

Now the next part isn't hard, but it takes a little trial and error if you don't know what you are doing. Slide the mainspring housing into the groove until it's holding in the bottom of the sear spring. Don't shove it all the way up, or you won't be able to get the grip safety in place. Of course, my method is to shove it all the way up and then back down about a quarter-inch. Slide the grip safety into place and then the mainspring housing up and it is all held in (generally) where it should go. What I suggest at this point is to put the safety pin into the hole at the top of the grip safety, but have the safety tab hanging off of the back of the gun. It leaves you room to manipulate the plunger spring. With all this in place, tap the pin at the bottom of the mainspring in.

Now is a good time to pull the hammer and let it down by pulling the trigger and gradually letting it go forward. It should be functioning just as it did before you took everything apart. Maybe better!

Slide the plunger spring into place; remember, the small end is forward. Of course, the spring pushes the rear of the plunger into the way of the safety. No worries. Use the firing pin or the side of a screwdriver to push it down while you wiggle the safety in. A little manipulation and it will snap into place.

The slide parts go back together just like that. Literally, do what you did to take it apart but in reverse order.

Now that your custom 1911 is back together, it's time to lube it. There are a million lubes on the market and many are outstanding. Are any better than the others? Probably, but since I lube my gun often, I don't have a preference. Bill Wilson is a fan of Ultima Lube, a product that he developed. I have used it and it works great. FrogLube is excellent, as well as, Miltec, Break-Free, and Ballistol. Pick your favorite. I recommend you put a tiny drop on the places where the safety and slide stop interact with your slide, and a generous amount in the slide rails. A pretty healthy amount should go on the barrel link, likewise the locking lugs of the barrel and the corresponding grooves in the slide. A little goes on the disconnector, near the tip, where the hammer and sear connect. I also recommend a goodly amount on the barrel where it slides in and out on the bushing.

Required maintenance is exactly that, maintenance required to keep your firearm in top condition, so you will have a dependable weapon or recreational tool at your disposal 24/7.

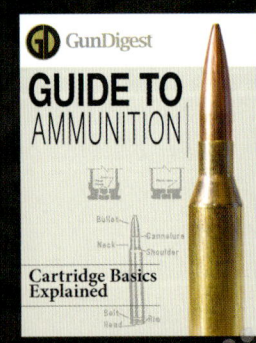
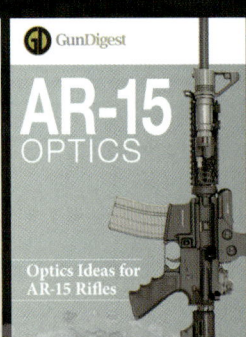
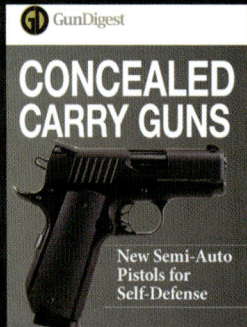